CW00403432

Series Editor *Urednica serije*
VERICA ZORIĆ

CROATIAN
phrase book and dictionary

Second edition *Drugo izdanje*
Prepared by *Priredile*
MIRJANA JURČIĆ
BERNADETTE KENDERIĆ
VERICA ZORIĆ

Zagreb, 2004.

Series Editor *Urednica biblioteke*
Verica Zorić

CROATIAN
phrase book and dictionary

Publisher *Nakladnik*
Naklada Ljevak

For the publisher *Za izdavača*
Zdenko Ljevak

Managing editor *Urednica-producent*
Verica Zorić

Croatian language adviser *Lektor za hrvatski jezik*
Nives Opačić

Reviewers *Recenzenti*
Nives Opačić
Gordana Vojvodić

Cover design *Vanjska oprema*
Borut Benčina

Typeset and layout *Slog i prijelom*
Studio Ljevak – Ana Pojatina

A CIP catalogue record is available from the National and University Library, Zagreb,
Croatia.
ISBN 953-178-478-7

The publication is registered by the *European Year of Languages (EYL 2001)*, organised
by the Council of Europe and the European Union, as one of the Croatian activities
to promote language learning and linguistic diversity in Europe. Activity name:
Quick bilingual guides to Croatian language: Croatian Language Souvenir (no. 689)

European Year of Languages 2001

Croatian Language Souvenir

Croatian Language Souvenir is a new series which promotes language diversities through bilingual dictionaries, a foreign language *and* Croatian as the target language. One of its primary goals is to promote the Croatian language which is one of the less widely used and less taught European languages.

The **Croatian Language Souvenir** series was launched in the *European Year of Languges 2001*. Each bilingual dictionary of the series serves not only as a quick guide to the Croatian language, but can also be used by students who are beginners in learning Croatian, or by visitors and tourists who wish to communicate in basic Croatian during their business trips or holiday in Croatia. The series is designed to encourage and support linguistic diversities throughout Europe, a priceless asset which must be protected. Therefore, through the **Croatian Language Souvenir** series, we intend to promote the cooperation and understanding between peoples who differ in languages, cultures and histories.

The **CROATIAN PHRASE BOOK AND DICTIONARY,** the book you are holding in your hands, is the first book in our **Croatian Language Souvenir** series. This English-Croatian edition offers a practical phrase book with both English-Croatian and Croatian-English dictionaries designed for English speakers of all ages, whether they are students, tourists or visitors. CROATIAN PHRASE BOOK AND DICTIONARY is divided into two main sections: the Phrase Book and the Dictionary. The Phrase Book presents typical situations and useful information pertinent to the Croatian language learner or tourist: the Croatian language, a basic grammar guide, a pronunciation guide, everyday phrases and words, arrival and departure, accommodation, at the tourist office, money, getting around, driving around Croatia, eating and drinking, shopping, services, postal and telecommunication services, sports, leisure and entertainment, health care and emergencies, and embassies. As implied by the title of the series, the edition is also meant to be a small keepsake, a memento of your stay in Croatia.

Did you know that, according to various demographic criteria used in establishing the number of Croatian speakers, around 7 million people in the world speak Croatian? Why not you?

For **Croatian Language Souvenir**
Verica Zorić

Hrvatski jezični suvenir

Biblioteka **Hrvatski jezični suvenir** njeguje jezične raznolikosti dvojezičnim rječnicima stranih jezika i hrvatskoga jezika, u kojima je ciljni jezik hrvatski, jezik koji se malo govori u Europi i svijetu, a još manje uči kao strani jezik.

Hrvatski jezični suvenir je nova serija/biblioteka pokrenuta u *Europskoj godini jezika 2001*. Tu govorimo o praktičnim dvojezičnim rječnicima - vodičima namijenjenim početnicima u učenju hrvatskoga jezika, kao i turistima u Hrvatskoj koji žele bolje razumjeti i ostvariti osnovnu komunikaciju na hrvatskom jeziku. Ovom serijom želimo očuvati europsku jezičnu raznolikost, suradnju i razumijevanje različitih jezika, kultura i povijesti.

CROATIAN PHRASE BOOK AND DICTIONARY, knjiga koju držite u rukama, prva je knjiga u biblioteci **Hrvatski jezični suvenir**. Englesko-hrvatsko izdanje praktični je rječnik hrvatskoga jezika namijenjen engleskim govornicima i turistima u Hrvatskoj, a ujedno i suvenir-rječnik, uspomena na boravak u Hrvatskoj. Ovaj Englesko-hrvatski i Hrvatsko-engleski rječnik sadrži posebno poglavlje u kojem su fraze svrstane po temama, kao što su: svakidašnje izreke, dolazak i odlazak, smještaj, u turističkoj agenciji, novac, upoznavanje grada/znamenitosti, putovanje Hrvatskom, jela i pića, kupovanje, razne usluge, poštanske i telekomunikacijske usluge, sportovi, slobodno vrijeme i zabave, zdravstvene usluge, veleposlanstva.

Koristeći se demografskim kriterijima pri utvrđivanju broja govornika hrvatskoga jezika, možemo pretpostaviti da hrvatski jezik govori oko 7 milijuna ljudi. Zašto ne biste i vi?

Za **Hrvatski jezični suvenir**
Verica Zorić

PREFACE

The ***Croatian Phrase Book and Dictionary*** is designed as a language guide for visitors to Croatia. This guide provides Croatian language assistance for a variety of situations in which visitors may find themselves while travelling in Croatia. The ***Croatian Phrase Book and Dictionary*** consists of two, user friendly parts.

The ***Phrase Book...***
- is divided into 16 units presenting typical situations relevant to travellers in a foreign country
- offers simple phrases and expressions without complicated grammatical structures
- offers basic and useful vocabulary
- gives the Croatian translation of the phrase and expression as well as its Croatian pronunciation transcription
- has a simple **Pronunciation Guide** based on English sounds to help pronounce Croatian in a fairly correct way
- offers practical and useful information which enables travellers to learn more about Croatia

The ***Dictionary...***
- has both **English-Croatian** and **Croatian-English** sections
- has over 2,000 words in each section
- provides words chosen to meet the needs of travellers
- serves as an easy reference when communicating with Croatian native speakers

No matter how you use this ***Croatian Phrase Book and Dictionary***, remember the following:

don't worry if you can't pronounce Croatian properly;
people will be very glad that you made the effort.

TABLE OF CONTENT

EMERGENCY TELEPHONE NUMBERS

Police 92
Fire. 93
Ambulance 94
Public Emergency Centre 985
Road Assistance. 987

USEFUL TELEPHONE NUMBERS

International Dialing Code for Croatia + Area Code +
Number . . . . 00 385 +
International Operator. 901
International Directory Enquiries 902
Directory Enquiries. 988
General Information 981
To Send a Telegram 96
Dialling the HTnet cell phone network 098
Dialling the VIPnet cell phone network 091
Croatian National Tourist Board . . . . . (01) 4699-333

AIRPORTS

Brač . . . . (021) 648-626
Dubrovnik . . . . (020) 773-333
Lošinj . . . . (051) 842-055
Osijek. . . . . (031) 297-340
Pula . . . . (052) 530-111
Rijeka . . . . (051) 842-035
Split . . . . (021) 203-506
Zadar . . . . (023) 313-311
Zagreb Pleso Airport. . . . . (01) 626-5222

How to start
THE CROATIAN LANGUAGE
CROATIAN GRAMMAR

PRONUNCIATION GUIDE
AND KEY

The Croatian Language

The Croatian language belongs to the Indo-European group of languages. These extend from India to Western Europe. Slavic languages are a sub-group within the Indo-European languages. The Proto-Slavic language group, which essentially refers to the period when all Slavs used the same language, lasted to approximately the 3rd century A.D. During this time, Slavs lived in a common homeland in the north-eastern areas of the Carpathian Mountains. In the 3rd century, the great migration of the Slav people began. As a result, the once shared Proto-Slavic language divided itself into three major groups:

- the East Slavic group
- the West Slavic group
- the South Slavic group (which includes Croatian).

The Croatian language has three dialects: 'Kajkavian', 'Chakavian' and 'Shtokavian'. The basis for the standard Croatian language is the 'Shtokavian' with a 'jekavian' pronunciation. The Croatian language uses the Latin alphabet.

Croatian Grammar

Fortunately, you don't need to learn the following material in order to survive in Croatia; however, those of you who wish to learn a little bit about Croatian grammar will perhaps find the explanations and notes both interesting and useful.

A Brief Summary of Croatian Grammar

The Croatian language has 30 letters: 5 vowels (a, e, i, o, u and sometimes r) and 25 consonants. We use the Latin alphabet; however, there are additional letters which do not exist in the Latin alphabet. They are: č, ć, dž, đ, lj, nj, š and ž. These letters are particular to the Croatian language and in general, to Slavic languages. Their pronunciation as well as stresses and accents are clearly shown and highlighted throughout this phrase book and dictionary. Suffice it to say, our phonetic transcription and stress marks will be easy for you to follow.

Nouns, Adjectives, Pronouns and Verbs

Nouns are words which name people, things, places and phenomena (for example: friend, window, park and heat). All nouns in Croatian have a gender: masculine, feminine and neutral. The majority of masculine nouns end in consonants while feminine nouns usually end in the letter -a (*žena* woman, *majka* mother). There are some feminine nouns which end in consonants such as *riječ* word and *stvar* thing. Neutral nouns end in the letters -o or -e such as *selo* village and *polje* field.

Croatian nouns have number (singular or plural) and declensions (seven cases) and change endings. Adjectives, pronouns and numbers can also be declined.

The cases are:
1. nominative (who? what? subject)
2. genitive (of whom? of what? possessive)
3. dative (to whom? to what? indirect object)
4. accusative (whom? what? direct object)
5. vocative
6. locative (about whom? about what?)
7. instrumental (with whom? with what?)

With some cases you will always find prepositions, while in other cases only the noun is required. The nominative case is always used without a preposition. It is the case most often used to indicate the subject of the predicate.

The following tables are declensions of masculine, feminine and neutral nouns with adjectives. These examples show the declensions of both nouns and adjectives.

Adjectives

Adjectives modify nouns by telling us for example the size, shape and relationship of a particular noun (pretty, wooden). Adjectives also have three genders like nouns since they are in essence an addition to the noun. Adjectives must agree in gender and in number with the noun they are modifying (nice flat **lijep** *stan* - masculine; beautiful woman **lijepa** *žena* - feminine; beautiful village **lijepo** *selo* - neutral). Adjectives are also declined but according to the declension valid for adjectives and pronouns which is different from the declension of nouns. For practical purposes, only the more frequently used definite adjective declensions are shown.

masculine	feminine	neutral
(hard-working son)	*(good actress)*	*(beautiful village)*
SINGULAR		

	masculine	feminine	neutral
N	marljivi sin	dobra glumica	lijepo selo
G	marljivog sina	dobre glumice	lijepog(a) sela
D	marljivom sinu	dobroj glumici	lijepom selu
A	marljivog sina	dobru glumicu	lijepo selo
V	marljivi sine	dobra glumice	lijepo selo
L	(o) marljivom sinu	(o) dobroj glumici	(o) lijepom selu
I	(s) marljivim sinom	(s) dobrom glumicom	(s) lijepim selom

PLURAL		

	masculine	feminine	neutral
N	marljivi sinovi	dobre glumice	lijepa sela
G	marljivih sinova	dobrih glumica	lijepih sela
D	marljivim sinovima	dobrim glumicama	lijepim selima
A	marljive sinove	dobre glumice	lijepa sela
V	marljivi sinovi	dobre glumice	lijepa sela
L	(o) marljivim sinovima	(o) dobrim glumicama	(o) lijepim selima
I	(s) marljivim sinovima	(s) dobrim glumicama	(s) lijepim selima

Warning: If a masculine noun designates a living thing, the genitive singular case is identical to the singular accusative case; if a masculine noun refers to a non-living thing then the nominative singular case is identical to the accusative case.

Pronouns

Pronouns replace nouns. There are many types of pronouns. We will deal with only a few. Personal pronouns are first, second and third persons (*ja, ti, on/ona/ono, mi vi oni/one/ona* I, you, he/she/it, we, you and they). These pronouns can have stressed or unstressed forms.

I	You	He, She, It
SINGULAR		
N ja	ti	on, ona, ono
G mene/me	tebe/te	njega/ga, nje/je, njega/ga
D meni/mi	tebi/ti	njemu/mu, njoj/joj, njemu/mu
A mene/me	tebe/te	njega/ga, nju/ju/je, njega/ga
V --------	ti	--------
L (o) meni	(o) tebi	(o) njemu, njoj, njemu
I sa mnom/ mnome	tobom	njim, njom, njim

We	You	They
PLURAL		
N mi	vi	oni, one, ona
G nas	vas	njih/ih
D nama/nam	vama/vam	njima/im
A nas	vas	njih/ih
V --------	vi	--------
L (o) nama	(o) vama	(o) njima
I (s) nama	(s) vama	(s) njima

Possessive pronouns (*moj, tvoj, njegov/njezin, naš, vaš, njihov* my, your, his/ her/ its, our, your and their) are declined like adjectives.

N moj	tvoj	njegov/njezin	naš	vaš	njihov
G mojeg	tvojeg	njegovog/njezinog	našeg	vašeg	njihovog
D mojem	tvojem	njegovom/njezinom	našem	vašem	njihovom
A mojeg	tvojeg	njegovog/njezinog	našeg	vašeg	njihovog
moj	tvoj	njegov/njezin	naš	vaš	njihov
V moj	tvoj	njegov/njezin	naš	vaš	njihov
L (o) mojem	tvojem	njegovom/njezinom	našem	vašem	njihovom
I (s) mojim	tvojim	njegovim/njezinim	našim	vašim	njihovim

The feminine and neutral gender of the singular forms and the plural of all genders are declined like adjectives (see Adjective Chart).

Pronouns used as demonstaratives: *ovaj (m.), ova (f.), ovo (n.)* this; *ovi (m.), ove (f.), ova (n.)* these; *onaj (m.), ona (f.), ono (n.)* that; *oni (m.), one (f.), ona (n.)* those.

N ovaj	ova	ovo	ovi	ove	ova
G ovog	ove	ovog	ovih	ovih	ovih
D ovom	ovoj	ovom	ovim	ovim	ovim
A ovog	ovu	ovo	ove	ove	ove
ovaj					
V ovaj	ova	ovo	ovi	ove	ova
L (o) ovom	ovoj	ovom	ovim	ovim	ovim
I (s) ovim	ovom	ovim	ovim	ovim	ovim

All other demonstrative pronouns are declined in the same manner (declination of adjectives and pronouns).

Verbs and Tenses

Tenses are used to show time and state of a particular action. Verbs are conjugated and are presented in first, second or third person (singular and plural). You can use pronouns in Croatian to indicate the subject of the predicate; however, this is not necessary since verb endings in Croatian already indicate the subject.

There are two auxiliary verbs in Croatian: *biti* (to be) and *htjeti* (will). These auxiliary verbs form tenses such as perfect or future tenses.

Present Tense

Auxiliary Verb: *biti* to be	
SINGULAR	
Stressed Form	*Unstressed Form*
1. jesam *(I am)*	sam *(I'm)*
2. jesi *(are)*	si *(you're)*
3. jest *(is)*	je *(he/she/it's)*
PLURAL	
1. jesmo *(we are)*	smo *(we're)*
2. jeste *(are)*	ste *(you're)*
3. jesu *(are)*	su *(they're)*

Auxiliary Verb: *htjeti* will	
SINGULAR	
Stressed Form	*Unstressed Form*
1. hoću *(I will)*	ću *(I'll)*
2. hoćeš	ćeš *(you'll)*
3. hoće	će *(he/she/it'll)*
PLURAL	
1. hoćemo *(we will)*	ćemo *(we'll)*
2. hoćete	ćete *(you'll)*
3. hoće	će *(they'll)*

The infinitive form of all the verbs in Croatian end in **-ti** or in **-ći** *(raditi, reći)*. We will only give you the endings of the present tense conjugation.

Present tense endings: *-am, -em, -im, -jem*

čitati *(to read)*	**tresti** *(to shake)*	**misliti** *(to think)*	**piti** *(to drink)*
SINGULAR			
1. (ja) čit**am**	tres**em**	misl**im**	pij**em**
2. (ti) čitaš	treseš	misliš	piješ
3. (on/ona/ono) čita	trese	misli	pije
PLURAL			
1. (mi) čitamo	tresemo	mislimo	pijemo
2. (vi) čitate	tresete	mislite	pijete
3. (oni/one/ona) čitaju	tresu	misle	piju

The root of the verb sometimes changes: there are phonetic changes depending on neighbouring vowels or consonants. We will not go into details here but give you only completed forms (examples: *pisati-pišem* write; *glodati-glođem* gnaw).

Past Tense

All past actions in Croatian, both continuous and simple, could be uttered in the *perfekt* the past tense.

The past tense is formed with the present tense of the auxiliary verb *biti* to be *(sam, si, je, smo, ste, su)* and the active past participle of the verb. This participle is formed by dropping the infinitive ending **-ti** and adding the appropriate gender ending which are as follows: masculine: **-o**; feminine: **-la**; neutral: **-lo**. The participle of *raditi* **work** would be formed like this: *radio, radila, radilo.*

---

to work: **raditi**

SINGULAR

1. ja sam radio/la/lo *(I worked/I was working)* or radio/la sam
2. ti si radio...   radio si...
3. on je radio...   radio je...

PLURAL

1. mi smo radili/le *(we worked/we were working)* radili/le smo...
2. vi ste radili...   radili ste...
3. oni su radili...   radili su...

Future Tense

The future tense is used to indicate actions about to happen or which will occur in the future. This tense in Croatian is formed with the present tense of the auxiliary verb **htjeti** (*ću, ćeš, će, ćemo, ćete, će*) and the infinitive form of the verb.

SINGULAR

1. ja ću raditi *(I will work)*
2. ti ćeš raditi
3. on, ona, ono će raditi

PLURAL

1. mi ćemo raditi *(we will work)*
2. vi ćete raditi
3. oni, one, ona će raditi

If you want to omit the pronoun, which can be done since the verb endings indicate the specific gender and number, then the infinitive of the main verb is placed before the present tense of the auxiliary verb, but in a contracted form.

SINGULAR | PLURAL

SINGULAR	PLURAL
1. radit ću *(I will work)*	**1.** radit ćemo *(we will work)*
2. radit ćeš	**2.** radit ćete
3. radit će	**3.** radit ćemo

Negative form

The negative particle/word **ne** *not* is always written before the verb and always as a separate word (examples: **ne** *znam* I do not know, **ne** *vidim* I do not see) even though it is often spoken as one word. The negative form is written as one form only in exceptional cases (**nemam** I don't have, **nisam** I am not, **neću** I will not, can be also written as **ne** *ću*).

There are exceptions to this rule:

imati	biti	htjeti
imam *(I have)*	ja sam *(I am)*	ja hoću *(I will)*
nemam *(I don't have)*	**ni**sam *(I'm not)*	**ne**ću (**ne** ću) *(I will not)*

Pronunciation Guide and Key

Croatian spelling is phonetic. Almost every letter is written exactly as it is pronounced. The exceptions are the two letters in *dž*, *lj* and *nj*. These are pronounced as one sound. The stressed syllable is printed in bold type.

Croatian Alphabet	Sounds like the...		Symbols
a	a in...	*father*	*a*
b	b in...	*bank*	*b*
c	ts in...	*boots*	*ts*
č and ć	ch in...	*chair*	*ch*
d	d in...	*dance*	*d*
dž and đ	j in...	*jam*	*j*
e	e in...	*bed*	*e*
f	f in ...	*five*	*f*
g	g in...	*go*	*g*
h	h in...	*hotel*	*h*
i	e/ee/ea in...	*me, see, please*	*ee*
j	y in...	*yes*	*y*
k	c/k in...	*cake*	*k*
l	l in...	*land*	*l*
lj	lio in..	*million*	*ly*
m	m in...	*man*	*m*
n	n in...	*no*	*n*
nj	nio in...	*onion*	*ny*
o	o/ou in...	*more, four*	*o*
p	p in...	*park*	*p*
r	r in...	*restaurant*	*r*
s	s in...	*sun*	*s*
š	sh in...	*fish*	*sh*
t	t in...	*towel*	*t*
u	oo in...	*pool*	*oo*
v	v in...	*van*	*v*
z	z in...	*zoo*	*z*
ž	s in...	*measure*	*zh*

Greetings

Good morning.
(until about 10:00 a.m.)
Good day/afternoon.
(10:00 a.m. to about
7:00 p.m.)
Good evening.
(from 7:00 p.m. on)
Good night.
(taking leave at night)
Hello/Hi!
So long.
Goodbye.
See you soon.

Pozdravi

Dobro jutro! *dobro yootro*

Dobar dan! *dobar dan*

Dobra večer! *dobra vecher*

Laku noć! *lakoo noch*

Bog/Zdravo! *bog/zdravo*
Doviđenja! *doveejenya*
Zbogom! *zbogom*
Do skorog viđenja!
do skorog veejenya

Basic Expressions

Yes/No
Please.
Thank you.
No, thank you.
I'm sorry.
You're welcome/Never mind.
It's OK.
What a pity!
Excuse me please/Pardon me.
Pardon/Sorry?
Just a minute, please.

Here you are.

Osnovni izrazi

Da/Ne *da/ne*
Molim! *moleem*
Hvala! *hvala*
Hvala, ne. *hvala ne*
Žao mi je. *zhao mee ye*
Ništa za to. *neeshta zato*
U redu je. *oo redoo ye*
Koja šteta! *koya shteta*
Oprostite! *oprosteete*
Molim? *moleem*
Samo tren, molim! *samo tren moleem*
Izvolite! *eezvoleete*

Thanks for your help.	**Hvala na pomoći.**
	hvala na pomochee
How are you?	**Kako ste?** *kako ste*
Fine.	**Izvrsno.** *eezvrsno*
Not bad.	**Nije loše.** *neeye loshe*
I'd like ...	**Htio/Htjela bih ...**
	hteeo/htyela beeh
I want/I don't want ...	**Želim/ne želim ...**
	zheleem/ne zheleem

Frequent Questions — Česta pitanja

What is this?	**Što je to?** *shto ye to*
Where is ...?	**Gdje je ...?** *gdye ye*
When?	**Kada?** *kada*
Who is ...?	**Tko je ...?** *tko ye*
Why?	**Zašto?** *zashto*
How much/many?	**Koliko?** *koleeko*
Is/Are there ...?	**Ima li ... ?** *eema lee*
Can I have ...?	**Mogu li dobiti ...?** *mogoo*
	lee dobeetee
What should I do?	**Što trebam napraviti?**
	shto trebam napraveetee

Communication Problems — Problemi u komunikaciji

I don't understand.	**Ne razumijem.**
	ne razoomeeyem
I don't speak Croatian.	**Ne govorim hrvatski.**
	ne govoreem hrvatskee

Can you help me?

Možete li mi pomoći?
mozhete lee mee pomochee

Please speak more slowly.

Govorite polakše!
govoreete polakshe

What does that mean?

Što to znači? *shto to*
znachee

Do you understand me?

Razumijete li me?
razoomeeyete lee me

Tell me once more.

Recite mi još jednom!
retseete mee yosh yednom

Could you explain this to me?

Možete li mi to objasniti?
mozhete lee mee to
obyasneetee

What do you call this?

Kako se to zove? *kako se*
to zove

Could you write it down?

Možete li mi to napisati?
mozhete lee mee to
napeesatee

Social Contacts

Druženje

My name is ...

Zovem se ... *zovem se*

What's your name?

Kako se vi zovete? *kako*
se vee zovete

This is my daughter Ann.

To je moja kći Ann. *to ye moya kchee an*

Is this Mr/Mrs ...?

Je li to gospodin/ gospođa ...? *ye lee to gospodeen/gospoja*

My husband isn't here.

Moj suprug nije tu. *moy sooproog neeye too*

My son is at the beach.

Moj sin je na plaži. *moy seen ye na plazhee*

I'd like to meet Miss ...

Htio/Htjela bih upoznati gospođicu ... *hteeo/htyela beeh oopoznatee gospojeetsoo*

Let me introduce you to Mr ...

Dopustite da vas predstavim gospodinu ... *dopoosteete da vas predstaveem gospodinoo*

I'd like to introduce Mrs ... to you.

Želim vam predstaviti gospođu ... *zheleem vam predstaveetee gospojoo*

Pleased to meet you.

Drago mi je što sam vas upoznao/la. *drago mee ye shto sam vas oopoznao/la*

I hope I'll see you again.

Nadam se da ću vas ponovno vidjeti. *nadam se da choo vas ponovno veedyetee*

Expressions of Time

Izražavanje vremena

day	**dan** *dan*
today	**danas** *danas*
tomorrow	**sutra** *sootra*
yesterday	**jučer** *yoocher*
morning	**jutro** *yootro*
in the morning	**ujutro** *ooyootro*
at noon	**u podne** *oo podne*
in the afternoon	**popodne** *popodne*
evening	**večer** *vecher*
in the evening	**navečer** *navecher*
night	**noć** *noch*
at night	**noću** *nochoo*
tonight	**večeras** *vecheras*
every day/daily	**svakog dana** *svakog dana*
week	**tjedan** *tyedan*
next week	**sljedeći tjedan** *slyedechee tyedan*
now	**sada** *sada*
always	**uvijek** *ooveeyek*
sometimes	**ponekad** *ponekad*
at the same time	**u isto vrijeme** *oo eesto vreeyeme*
soon	**uskoro** *ooskoro*
later on	**kasnije** *kasneeye*
never	**nikada** *neekada*

Days of the Week

Dani u tjednu

Monday	**ponedjeljak** *ponedyelyak*
Tuesday	**utorak** *ootorak*
Wednesday	**srijeda** *sreeyeda*
Thursday	**četvrtak** *chetvrtak*
Friday	**petak** *petak*
Saturday	**subota** *soobota*
Sunday	**nedjelja** *nedyelya*

Months

Mjeseci

January	**siječanj** *seeyechany*
February	**veljača** *velyacha*
March	**ožujak** *ozhooyak*
April	**travanj** *travany*
May	**svibanj** *sveebany*
June	**lipanj** *leepany*
July	**srpanj** *srpany*
August	**kolovoz** *kolovoz*
September	**rujan** *rooyan*
October	**listopad** *leestopad*
November	**studeni** *stoodenee*
December	**prosinac** *proseenats*

Seasons

Godišnja doba

spring	**proljeće** *prolyeche*
summer	**ljeto** *lyeto*
autumn/fall	**jesen** *yesen*
winter	**zima** *zeema*

Talking about the Weather

It's a lovely morning.

Jutro je divno. *yootro ye deevno*

Isn't the weather wonderful?

Nije li vrijeme krasno? *neeye lee vreeyeme krasno*

It's very hot today.

Danas je jako vruće. *danas ye yako vrooche*

Is it going to stay so warm?

Hoće li ostati tako toplo? *hoche lee ostatee tako toplo*

The breeze is refreshing.

Povjetarac osvježava. *povyetarats osvyezhava*

The evenings are cool.

Večeri su svježe. *vecheree soo svyezhe*

Is it going to rain soon?

Hoće li uskoro pasti kiša? *hoche lee ooskoro pastee keesha*

The storm was very strong last night.

Prošle noći bila je vrlo jaka oluja. *proshle nochee beela ye vrlo yaka olooya*

Colours

black

crn *tsrn*

blue

modar/plav *modar/plav*

brown

smeđ *smej*

green	**zelen** *zelen*
navy	**tamnomodar** *tamnomodar*
orange	**narančast** *naranchast*
purple	**ljubičast** *lyoobeechast*
red	**crven** *tsrven*
white	**bijel** *beeyel*
yellow	**žut** *zhoot*

0 zero	**nula** *noola*
1 one	**jedan** *yedan*
2 two	**dva** *dva*
3 three	**tri** *tree*
4 four	**četiri** *cheteeree*
5 five	**pet** *pet*
6 six	**šest** *shest*
7 seven	**sedam** *sedam*
8 eight	**osam** *osam*
9 nine	**devet** *devet*
10 ten	**deset** *deset*
11 eleven	**jedanaest** *yedanaest*
12 twelve	**dvanaest** *dvanaest*
13 thirteen	**trinaest** *treenaest*
14 fourteen	**četrnaest** *chetrnaest*
15 fifteen	**petnaest** *petnaest*
16 sixteen	**šesnaest** *shesnaest*
17 seventeen	**sedamnaest** *sedamnaest*
18 eighteen	**osamnaest** *osamnaest*
19 nineteen	**devetnaest** *devetnaest*
20 twenty	**dvadeset** *dvadeset*
21 twenty-one	**dvadeset i jedan** *dvadest ee yedan*

30 thirty	**trideset** *treedeset*
40 forty	**četrdeset** *chetrdeset*
50 fifty	**pedeset** *pedeset*
60 sixty	**šezdeset** *shezdeset*
70 seventy	**sedamdeset** *sedamdeset*
80 eighty	**osamdeset** *osamdeset*
90 ninety	**devedeset** *devedeset*
100 hundred	**sto** *sto*
101 a hundred and one	**sto i jedan** *sto ee yedan*
200 two hundred	**dvjesto** *dvyesto*
300 three hundred	**tristo** *treesto*
1000 thousand	**tisuća** *teesoocha*
2000 two thousand	**dvije tisuće** *dveeye teesooche*
first	**prvi** *prvee*
second	**drugi** *droogee*
third	**treći** *trechee*
fourth	**četvrti** *chetvrtee*
fifth	**peti** *petee*
a quarter	**(jedna) četvrtina** *(yedna) chetvrteena*
half a	**(jedna) polovica** *(yedna) poloveetsa*

Telling Time

Koliko je sati

What time is it, please?

Koliko je sati, molim?
koleeko ye satee moleem

It's 8 a.m. (morning)

8 je sati (ujutro). *osam ye satee (ooyootro)*

It's 3 p.m. (afternoon)

3 su sata (popodne). *tree soo sata (popodne)*

It's 8 p.m. (evening)	**8 je sati (navečer).** *osam ye satee (navecher)*
It's...	**Sada je ...** *sada ye*
8:00	**osam sati** *osam satee*
8:10	**osam i deset** *osam ee deset*
8:15	**osam i petnaest** *osam ee petnaest*
	(osam i četvrt) *osam ee chetvrt*
8:30	**osam i trideset** *osam ee treedeset*
	(pola devet) *pola devet*
8:45	**osam i četrdeset pet** *osam ee chetrdeset pet*
	(četvrt do devet) *chetvrt do devet*
8:50	**deset do devet** *deset do devet*

In formal speech, the 24-hour clock system is used.

The bus leaves at 2 p.m.	**Autobus polazi u 14 sati.** *aootoboos polazee u chetrnaest satee*

Having trouble
Ako ste u neprilici ili opasnosti

Help!	**Upomoć!** *oopomoch*
I can't breathe.	**Ne mogu disati.** *ne mogu deesatee*

Fire!	**Vatra!** *vatra*
Stop!	**Stoj!** *stoy*
I'll call police.	**Zvat ću policiju.** *zvat choo poleetseeyoo*
It's urgent.	**Hitno je.** *heetno ye*
I'm lost.	**Izgubio/izgubila sam se.** *eezgoobeeo/eezgoobeela* *sam se*
I lost my …	**Izgubio/izgubila sam …** *eezgoobeeo/eezgoobeela sam*
passport	**putovnicu** *pootovneetsoo*
car key	**ključ od auta** *klyooch od aoota*
mobile phone	**mobitel** *mobeetel*
glasses	**naočale** *naochale*
digital camera	**digitalni fotoaparat** *deegeetalnee fotoaparat*
I've been robbed.	**Opljačkali su me.** *oplyachkalee soo me*
They stole my …	**Ukrali su mi …** *ookralee soo mee*
car	**… auto** *aooto*
handbag	**… torbicu** *torbeetsoo*
wallet.	**… novčanik.** *novchaneek*

Arrival & Departure

Croatia can be reached by air, road, rail and sea. All foreigners are required to present a valid passport upon entering Croatia. Croatian entry/exit visas are required for certain countries. These can be procured upon arrival at the airport or at border crossings. Contact your local Croatian Embassy or Consulate for more information. All foreigners who have a valid driving licence or an international driving license are allowed to drive within Croatia. All airports, railway and coach (bus) stations, as well as most tourist agencies, provide information and services in English.

KEY WORDS

customs control	**carinska kontrola** *tsareenska kontrola*
duty free shop	**bescarinska prodavaonica** *bestsareenska prodavaoneetsa*
passport	**putovnica** *pootovneetsa*
reservation	**rezervacija** *rezervatseeya*
suitcase	**kofer** *kofer*
visa	**viza** *veeza*

At the Airport   U zračnoj luci

See **Useful Telephone Numbers** for list of airports in Croatia.

KEY WORDS

airplane	**zrakoplov** *zrakoplov*
airport	**zračna luka** *zrachna looka*
flight	**let** *let*

Arrival

Dolazak

I have a/an … passport
Imam … putovnicu
eemam … pootovneetsu

American **američku** *amereechkoo*
Australian **australsku** *aoostralskoo*
British **britansku** *breetanskoo*
Canadian **kanadsku** *kanadskoo*

Do I need a Croatian visa?
Trebam li hrvatsku vizu?
trebam lee hrvatskoo veezoo

Where can I get it?
Gdje ju mogu dobiti?
gdye yoo mogoo dobeetee

My child is registered in my passport.
Moje dijete upisano je u moju putovnicu. *moye deeyete oopeesano je oo moyoo pootovneetsu*

I have nothing to declare.
Nemam što prijaviti.
nemam shto preeyaveetee

I have …
a bottle of whiskey

a carton of cigarettes
Imam … *eemam*
bocu viskija *botsoo veeskeeya*
šteku cigareta *shtekoo tseegareta*

This laptop is for my personal use.
Ovaj laptop je za moju uporabu. *ovaj laptop ye za moyoo ooporaboo*

Do I have to declare my video camera?

Moram li prijaviti svoju videokameru? *moram lee preeyaveetee svoyoo veedeokameroo*

Where is the information office?

Gdje se mogu dobiti informacije? *gdye se mogoo dobeetee eenformatseeye*

At what time is the connecting flight to Dubrovnik?

Kada je let za Dubrovnik? *kada ye let za doobrovneek*

Where can I change money?

Gdje mogu promijeniti novac? *gdye mogoo promeeyeneetee novats*

Where can I get a bus into the city?

Gdje stoji autobus za grad? *gdye stoyee aootoboos za grad*

Where are the taxis?

Gdje stoji taksi? *gdye stoyee taksee*

Where can I rent a car?

Gdje mogu rentirati auto? *gdye mogoo renteeratee aooto*

Departure

Odlazak

Where is the Croatian Airlines check-in counter?

Gdje se prijavljuje let za Croatia Airlines? *gdye se preeyavlyooye let za* Croatia Airlines

I need to change my reservation.

Trebam promijeniti rezervaciju. *trebam promeeyeneetee rezervatseeyoo*

When is the next flight to…?

Kada je sljedeći let za…? *kada ye slyedechee let za*

May I have a schedule of flights to…?

Mogu li dobiti red letenja za…? *mogoo lee dobeetee red letenya za*

I would like to make reservations to…

Želim rezervaciju za… *zheleem rezervatseeyu za*

I need a Business/Economy ticket to…

Trebam kartu za business/turističku klasu za… *trebam kartoo za business/tooreesteechkoo klasoo za*

I would like an aisle/window seat.

Molim vas sjedalo do prolaza/prozora. *moleem vas syedalo do prolaza/prozora*

I have two suitcases.

Imam dva kofera. *eemam dva kofera*

41

I need boarding assistance.	**Trebam pomoć pri ulazu u zrakoplov.** *trebam* *pomoch pree oolazoo oo zrakoplov*
Where is the duty free shop?	**Gdje je djutić?** *gdye ye djootich*

Na autobusnom/ željezničkom kolovoru

The coach (bus) system in Croatia is quite good. Most companies offer first class vehicles with express routes to major cities and towns across Croatia. The train system is not as convenient, but it is getting better. Both train and coach services offer direct lines to major European cities. Dial **988** (Directory Assistance) to get the number of your nearest coach/railway station.

KEY WORDS

coach (bus)	**autobus** *aootoboos*
coach/railway station	**autobusni/željeznički kolodvor** *aootoboosnee/ zhelyezneechkee kolodvor*
one-way ticket	**karta u jednom smjeru** *karta oo yednom smyeroo*
return ticket	**povratna karta** *povratna karta*
train	**vlak** *vlak*

When is the next coach/train to…?	**Kada polazi sljedeći autobus/vlak za…?** *kada polazee slyedechee aootoboos/vlak za*
I need a schedule to…	**Treba mi vozni red za…** *treba mee voznee red za*
I need a return/one-way ticket to…	**Trebam povratnu kartu/kartu u jednom smjeru za…** *trebam povratnoo kartoo/kartoo oo yednom smyeroo za*
I want to reserve a seat.	**Želim rezervirati sjedalo.** *zheleem rezerveeratee syedalo*
I need a first/second class ticket to…	**Trebam kartu prvog/drugog razreda za…** *trebam kartoo prvog/droogog razreda za*
How much is a ticket to…?	**Koliko košta karta za…?** *koleeko koshta karta za*
Is there a dining car on the train?	**Ima li vagon restoran u ovom vlaku?** *eema lee vagon restoran oo ovom vlakoo*
Are there toilet facilities on board?	**Postoji li toalet u autobusu?** *postoyee lee toalet oo aootoboosoo*
Do I need to change coaches/trains?	**Moram li presjedati?** *moram lee presyedatee*

When do we arrive in...?	**Kada stižemo u...?** *kada steezhemo oo*
Is this the coach/train to...?	**Je li ovo autobus/vlak za...?** *ye lee ovo aootoboos/vlak za*
Is this seat taken?	**Je li ovo mjesto zauzeto?** *ye lee ovo myesto zaoozeto*

Ferry Travel/Ship Travel

Putovanje trajektom/brodom

Jadroagent and **Jadrolinija** are the two major ferry companies in Croatia. Some ferry routes require reservations, while most operate on a 'first come' basis. Other ferry companies such as **Atlas** and **Dalmacijaturist** take reservations and offer ferry or hydrofoil services for passengers only. Dial **988** (Directory Assistance) to get the number of the company nearest you. To avoid frustration and long queues, inform yourself well in advance about delays by calling **987** (Road Assistance.)

KEY WORDS

cabin	**kabina** *kabeena*
ferry	**trajekt** *trayekt*
hydrofoil	**hidrogliser** *heedrogleeser*
port	**luka** *looka*
ship	**brod** *brod*

Where is the port?

Gdje je luka? *gdye ye looka*

At what time is the next sailing?

Kada polazi sljedeći brod za...? *kada polazee slyedechee brod za*

When do we board?

Kada počinje ukrcaj na brod? *kada pocheenye ukrtsay na brod*

I need a ticket for one car, two adults and one child.

Trebam kartu za auto, dvoje odraslih i jedno dijete. *trebam kartoo za aooto dvoye odrasleeh ee yedno deeyete*

I would like to reserve a cabin.

Želio/Željela bih rezervirati kabinu. *zheleeo/zhelyela beeh rezerveeratee kabeenoo*

How long is the crossing?

Koliko traje plovidba? *koleeko traye ploveedba*

Is there a restaurant on board?

Postoji li na trajektu restoran? *postoyee lee na trayektoo restoran*

At which pier is the ferry docked?

Gdje pristaje trajekt? *gdye preestaye trayekt*

When do I need to be at the pier?

Kad trebam biti na pristaništu? *kad trebam beetee na preestaneeshtoo*

Marinas

Marine

Croatia's picturesque Adriatic coastline is serviced by many marinas. All marinas provide a wide range of facilities and services. Besides the usual reception services, most marinas provide restaurants, toilet, shower and laundry facilities, repair shops and stores. If you spend your holidays cruising the blue Adriatic, you'll find all the marinas as well as Croatia's thousand islands plotted on your navigation maps.

KEY WORDS

berth	**vez** *vez*
boat	**brod** *brod*
bow	**pramac** *pramats*
cast anchor	**baciti sidro** *batseetee seedro*
dock/pier	**pristanište** *preestaneeshte*
fender	**bokobran** *bokobran*
harbour	**luka** *looka*
low tide/high tide	**oseka/plima** *oseka/pleema*
port side	**lijevi bok** *leeyevee bok*
sailboat/sailing boat	**jedrilica** *yedreeleetsa*
speedboat	**gliser** *gleeser*
starboard	**desni bok** *desnee bok*
stern	**krma** *krma*

I need a berth for two days.

Treba mi vez na dva dana. *treba mee vez na dva dana*

Does the berth have a water and power supply?

Ima li vez vodu i struju? *eema lee vez vodoo ee strooyo*

Is your marina opened year round?

Je li vaša marina otvorena cijele godine? *ye lee vasha mareena otvorena tseeyele godeene*

What is your pier's sea depth?

Koja je dubina na pristaništu? *koya ye doobeena na preestaneeshtoo*

Do you have space on land?

Imate li vez na suhom? *eemate lee vez na soohom*

Does your marina have a 15 ton crane?

Ima li vaša marina petnaesttonsku dizalicu? *eema lee vasha mareena petnaesttonskoo deezaleetsoo*

What are your rates?

Kolike su vaše pristojbe? *koleeke soo vashe preestoybe*

Is there a sheltered harbour nearby?

Postoji li u blizini zaštićena luka? *postoyee lee oo bleezeenee zashteechena looka*

Where can I moor my boat?

Gdje mogu privezati brod? *gdye mogoo preevezatee brod*

Where can I buy nautical gear?

Gdje mogu kupiti nautičku opremu? *gdye mogoo koopeetee naootichkoo opremoo*

Where can I have repairs done?	**Gdje mogu obaviti popravak?** *gdye mogoo obaveetee popravak*
Where is the port authority office?	**Gdje je lučka kapetanija?** *gdye ye loochka kapetaneeya*

Car Rental   Rent-a-car

Car rental companies are located at all airports and major hotels. Most cities and towns also have car rental companies. Be sure to fully inform yourself regarding rates and insurance.

KEY WORDS

car	**automobil** *aootomobeel*
rent	**unajmiti** *oonaymeetee*
van	**kombi** *kombee*

Where can I rent a car/van?	**Gdje mogu unajmiti automobil/kombi?** *gdye mogoo oonaymeetee aootomobeel/kombee*
I need a small/large car.	**Trebam mali/veliki automobil.** *trebam malee/veleekee aootomobeel*
What is the daily rate?	**Kolika je cijena po danu?** *koleeka ye tseeyena po danoo*

Is there a charge per kilometre?

Naplaćuje li se i po kilometru? *naplachooye lee se ee po keelometroo*

Is petrol (gas) included?

Je li benzin uključen? *ye lee benzeen ooklyoochen*

I would like to leave the car in...

Želim ostaviti automobil u... *zheleem ostaveetee aootomobeel u*

I need a rented car with chauffeur.

Želim auto sa šoferom. *zheleem aooto sa shoferom*

How much is insurance?

Koliko stoji osiguranje? *koleeko stoyee oseegooranye*

Lost Luggage   Izgubljena prtljaga

All airports, railway and coach stations have a lost/damaged luggage office.

bag	**torba** *torba*
luggage	**prtljaga** *prtlyaga*
suitcase	**kofer** *kofer*

Where is the luggage from the Manchester flight?

Gdje je prtljaga s leta iz Manchestera? *gdye ye prtlyaga s leta eez manchestera*

Where is the lost luggage office?	**Gdje je ured za izgubljenu prtljagu?** *gdye ye oored za eezgooblyenoo prtlyagoo*
My suitcase has been damaged.	**Moj je kofer oštećen.** *moy ye kofer oshtechen*
My luggage has not arrived.	**Moja prtljaga nije stigla.** *moya prtlyaga neeye steegla*
Can you forward my luggage to Hotel…?	**Možete li poslati moju prtljagu u hotel…?** *mozhete lee poslatee moyoo prtlyagoo oo hotel*

Accomodation

If you plan to go to Croatia on your own, get information beforehand about the place where you intend to stay and book accomodation in advance. This can be done at your local travel agency or by visiting www.htz.hr the Croatian Tourist Board web-site. Hotels used to be classified by the letters A, B and C. A category hotels = excellent, B = very good, and C = fairly good hotels. The familiar 3-star, 4-star and 5-star grading system has recently been introduced in Croatia. *Bed and Breakfast* accomodation called pansion **pansion** *panseeon* are usually 2-star hotel category. There are apartments **apartmani** *apartmanee* for rent as well as rooms **sobe** *sobe* in private houses. Ask if breakfast is included in the price of the room. Regarding the meals at the place where you are staying, you could have full board **puni pansion** *poonee panseeon* with three meals a day, or half board **polupansion** *poloopanseeon* with breakfast and lunch or dinner. See **At the Tourist Office** (p. 61) for more information regarding renting accommodation.

KEY WORDS

car park	**parkiralište** *parkeeraleeshte*
double room	**dvokrevetna soba** *dvokrevetna soba*
hotel	**hotel** *hotel*
reception desk	**recepcija** *retseptseeya*
reservation	**rezervacija** *rezervatseeya*
single room	**jednokrevetna soba** *yednokrevetna soba*

Checking in

Prijava boravka

Could you direct me to
the ... Hotel, please?

**Možete li me uputiti do
hotela ...?** *mozhete lee me
oopooteetee do hotela*

My name is ...
I've a reservation for today.

**Zovem se ...
Imam rezervaciju od
danas.** *zovem se eemam
rezervatseeyu od danas*

I've booked a room for
three nights.

**Rezervirao/la sam sobu za
tri noći.** *rezerveerao/la sam
soboo za tree nochee*

Could I have a room ...?

Mogu li dobiti sobu ...?
mogoo lee dobeetee soboo

    with a balcony
    facing the park

    s balkonom *s balkonom*
    prema parku *prema
    parkoo*

    with a sea view

    s pogledom na more
    s pogledom na more

Is there a lift (elevator) in
the building?

Ima li zgrada lift? *eema lee
zgrada lift*

Can I have the room on
a lower floor?

**Mogu li dobiti sobu na
nižem katu?** *mogoo lee
dobeetee soboo na neezhem
katoo*

Could I have a quieter
room?

**Mogu li dobiti mirniju
sobu?** *mogoo lee dobeetee
meerneejoo soboo*

Where is the restaurant? **Gdje je restoran?** *gdye ye restoran*

Where can I find the chamber maid? **Gdje mogu naći sobaricu?** *gdye mogoo nachee sobareetsoo*

At what time do you serve ...? **U koliko sati poslužujete ...?** *oo koleeko satee posloozhooyete*

  breakfast **doručak** *doroochak*
  lunch **ručak** *roochak*
  dinner **večeru** *vecheroo*

Can I have the key? **Mogu li dobiti ključ?** *mogoo lee dobeetee klyooch*

The room number is ... **Broj sobe je ...** *broy sobe ye*

Private Accomodation   Privatni smještaj

KEY WORDS

apartment	**apartman** *apartman*
bed and breakfast	**pansion** *pansion*
room	**soba** *soba*

Do you have a vacant room? **Imate li slobodnu sobu?** *eemate lee slobodnu soboo*

I'd like a double room with a ...

Želio/Željela bih dvokrevetnu sobu ... *zheleeo/zhelyela beeh dvokrevetnoo soboo*

| shower | **s tušem** *s tooshem* |
| bathroom | **s kupaonicom** *s koopaoneetsom* |

What is the price ...?

Koliko stoji soba ...? *koleeko stojee soba*

per person	**po osobi** *po osobee*
per night	**za noć** *za noch*
for a week	**na tjedan** *na tyedan*

Is breakfast included in the price?

Je li doručak uključen u cijenu? *ye lee doroochak ooklyoochen oo ceeyenoo*

Can I see the room?

Mogu li vidjeti sobu? *mogoo lee veedyetee soboo*

The room is too small. Could I have a bigger one?

Soba je premala. Mogu li dobiti veću? *soba ye premala mogoo lee dobeetee vechoo*

The room at the back would be better.

Soba odostraga bila bi bolja. *soba odostraga beela bee bolya*

This room will do.

Ova je soba u redu. *ova ye soba oo redoo*

Is there a car park nearby? | **Je li parkiralište u blizini?**
ye lee parkeeraleeshte oo bleezeenee

Are pets allowed? | **Primate li kućne ljubimce?** *preemate lee koochne lyoobeemtse*

Requests and Complaints

Zamolbe i pritužbe

KEY WORDS

chamber maid	**sobarica** *sobareetsa*
manager	**direktor** *deerektor*
receptionist	**recepcioner** *retseptseeoner*

Could you help me with the luggage? | **Možete li mi pomoći s prtljagom?** *mozhete lee mee pomochee s prtlyagom*

The bed isn't comfortable. | **Krevet nije udoban.** *krevet neeye oodoban*

I need another...
pillow

hanger

glass

| **Trebam još...** *trebam yosh*
jedan jastuk *yedan yastook*
jednu vješalicu *yednoo vyeshaleetsoo*
jednu čašu *yednoo chashoo*

The … doesn't work.	**Ne radi …** *ne radee*
air-conditioner	**klima.** *kleema*
night lamp	**noćna lampa.** *nochna lampa*

There's no toilet paper in the bathroom.	**Nema toaletnog papira u kupaonici.** *nema toaletnog papeera oo koopaoneetsee*

The sink is clogged.	**Umivaonik je začepljen.** *oomivaonik ye zacheplyen*

The tap is dripping.	**Pipa curi.** *peepa tsooree*

The bathtub is clogged.	**Kada je začepljena.** *kada ye zacheplyena*

The curtains can't be drawn.	**Zavjese se ne mogu povući.** *zavyese se ne mogoo povoochee*

There's no hot water.	**Nema tople vode.** *nema tople vode*

Something is wrong with the TV.	**Nešto nije u redu s televizorom.** *neshto neeye oo redoo s televeezorom*

Can you fix it?	**Možete li to popraviti?** *mozhete lee to popraveetee*

Checking Out   Odjava boravka

bill	**račun** *rachoon*
cash	**gotovina** *gotoveena*
credit card	**kreditna kartica** *kredeetna karteetsa*

I'm leaving tomorrow. — **Sutra odlazim.** *sootra odlazeem*

What is the check-out time? — **U koje vrijeme moram isprazniti sobu?** *oo koye vreeyeme moram eesprazneetee soboo*

I'd like to pay my bill. — **Htio/Htjela bih platiti račun.** *hteeo/htyela beeh plateetee rachoon*

I'll pay with my credit card. — **Platit ću kreditnom karticom.** *plateet choo kredeetnom karteetsom*

I'll pay cash. — **Platit ću gotovinom.** *plateet choo gotoveenom*

I've enjoyed staying at your place. — **Boravak ovdje bio je pravi užitak.** *boravak ovdye beeo ye pravee oozheetak*

Thanks for everything. — **Hvala na svemu.** *hvala na svemoo*

Camping   Kampiranje

There are many campgrounds along the Adriatic coast as well as in the interior of Croatia. Services offered range from the very simple to the extremely well organized.

campground	**kamp** *kamp*
campground pass	**propusnica za kamp**
	propoosneetsa za **kamp**
drinking water	**voda za piće** *voda za* **peeche**
electric power	**električna struja** *elektreechna* **strooya**

Have you got room for the ...?	**Imate li mjesta za ...?**
	eemate lee myesta za
tent	**šator** *shator*
trailer	**prikolicu** *preekoleetsoo*
RV	**karavan** *karavan*
mobile home	**kamp kućicu** *kamp koocheetsoo*

How much does it cost per ...?	**Koliko košta po ...?**
	koleeko koshta po
person	**osobi** *osobee*
day	**danu** *danoo*

We would like to stay ... days.	**Rado bi ostali ... dana.**
	rado bee ostalee ... dana

Is there a ...?	**Ima li tu ...?** *eema lee too*
store	**prodavaonica**
	prodavaoneetsa
restaurant	**restoran** *restoran*

Are there laundry facilities?

Postoji li mogućnost pranja rublja? *postoyee lee mogoochnost pranya rooblya*

Where are the ...?
   toilets
   showers

Gdje su ...? *gdye soo*
   zahodi *zahodee*
   tuševi *tooshevee*

Is there a security guard at night?

Ima li kamp noćne čuvare? *eema lee kamp nochne choovare*

When do the gates close at night?

Kad se kamp navečer zatvara? *kad se kamp navecher zatvara*

Please show me my parking spot.

Molim vas, pokažite mi moje mjesto za parkiranje. *moleem vas pokazheete mee moye myesto za parkeeranye*

At the tourist office

RENTING ACCOMODATION

EXCURSIONS

There are many tourist agencies in all resort areas and major cities which offer services and advice for renting accommodation, excursions, public transport, local events and even exchange rates if needed. See also **Accomodation** and **Sports, Leisure and Entertainment** for more information.

Renting Accommodation

Unajmljivanje

KEY WORDS

kitchenette	**kuhinjica** *koo*heenyeetsa
landlady	**vlasnica** *vlas*neetsa
landlord	**vlasnik** *vlas*neek
move in	**useliti se** *oos*eleetee se
shared bathroom	**zajednička kupaonica** *za*yedneechka koopaoneetsa

---

Can you help us, please?	**Molim vas, pomozite nam.** *mol*eem vas pomo*zeetee* nam
Could we get a room for one night?	**Možemo li dobiti sobu za jednu noć?** *mo*zhemo lee do*beetee* so*boo* za *jed*noo **noch**
We are looking for a quiet room.	**Tražimo mirnu sobu.** tra*zheemo* **meer***noo* so*boo*
How much is the room per night?	**Koliko stoji soba na noć?** ko*leeko* sto*yee* so*ba* na noch

We need an apartment for a week.	**Treba nam apartman na tjedan dana.** *treba nam apartman na tyedan dana*
How many rooms are there?	**Koliko ima soba?** *koleeko eema soba*
We are a family of four.	**Mi smo četveročlana obitelj.** *mee smo chetverochlana obeetely*
Are the rooms air-condioned?	**Je li u sobama klimatski uređaj?** *ye lee oo sobama kleematskee oorejay*
Is the kitchenette fully equipped?	**Je li kuhinjica potpuno opremljena?** *ye lee kooheenyeetsa potpuno opremlyena*
We don't want it with ...	**Nećemo sa ...** *nechemo sa*
a shared bathroom	**zajedničkom kupaonicom** *zayedneechkom koopaoneetsom*
a sofa bed	**sofom za spavanje** *sofom za spavanye*
Is it near the beach?	**Je li blizu plaže?** *ye lee bleezoo plazhe*
When could we see the apartment?	**Kada možemo vidjeti apartman?** *kada mozhemo veedyetee apartman*

Could we move in soon?	**Možemo li se odmah useliti?** *mozhemo lee se odmah ooseleetee*
Is it far from here?	**Je li daleko odavde?** *ye lee daleko odavde*
How do we get there?	**Kako možemo doći onamo?** *kako mozhemo dochee onamo*
Can I park nearby?	**Mogu li se parkirati u blizini?** *mogoo lee se parkeeratee oo bleezeenee*

Excursions   Izleti

Croatia is…

…spectacular natural beauty from its mountains, canyons, valleys and hinterlands to its unspoiled coastline dotted with over 1,000 islands…

…cathedrals, castles and ancient cities from the Roman wine cellars in Ilok and the spires of Zagreb's cathedral to the treasures of Zadar, and Pula's amphitheatre…

…time-honoured traditions and world class festivals from the *Alka* in Sinj to the *Dubrovnik Summer Arts Festival*…

…national parks with flora and fauna unique in the world from the wonders of the Plitvice lakes to the Velebit peaks.

It's all yours to discover. Travel agencies and tourist offices organise half or full day tours to places worth seeing. Ask for brochures!

KEY WORDS

brochure	**brošura** *broshoora*
guided tour	**izlet s vodičem** *eezlet s vodeechem*
national park	**nacionalni park** *natseeonalnee park*
tour bus	**izletnički autobus** *eezletneechkee aootoboos*

We'd like to make a trip to ...	**Htjeli bismo otići na izlet do ...** *htyelee beesmo oteechee na eezlet do*
Have you got any brochures about it?	**Imate li kakvih brošura o tomu?** *eemate lee kakveeh broshoora o tomoo*
I'd like to make a half-day sightseeing tour to...	**Htio/Htjela bih napraviti poludnevni izlet u...** *hteeo/htyela beeh napraveetee poloodnevnee eezlet oo*
Will there be a tour guide?	**Hoćemo li imati vodiča?** *hochemo lee eematee vodeecha*
Can we go there by ..?	**Možemo li ići ...?** *mozhemo lee eechi*
bus	**autobusom** *aootoboosom*
boat	**brodom** *brodom*
hydrofoil	**gliserom** *gleeserom*

When does the tour bus leave?	**Kad polazi izletnički autobus?** *kad polazee eezletnichkee aootoboos*
Where does the tour bus depart from?	**Odakle polazi izletnički autobus?** *odakle polazee eezletneechkee aootoboos*
How long does it take to get there?	**Koliko se putuje?** *koleeko se pootooye*
When does the boat arrive in ...?	**Kada stiže brod u ...?** *kada steezhe brod oo*
Where does the boat dock?	**Gdje brod pristaje?** *gdye brod preestaye*
When do we get back?	**Kada se vraćamo?** *kada se vrachamo*
How much is the ticket for the excursion to ...?	**Koliko košta karta za izlet u ...?** *koleeko koshta karta za eezlet oo*

Money

The main Croatin currency is called **kuna** *koona*. Croatian notes come in denominations of 10, 20, 50, 100, 200, 500, and 1000 **kuna**. Coins come in denominations of 1, 2, 5 and 25 **kuna**. There are also 1, 2, 5, 10, 20, and 50 **lipa** *leepa* coins. Foreign currency can be changed at airports, rail and bus stations, post offices, banks, major hotels, and exchange offices. Exchange offices usually offer better exchange rates. You may want to check the Croatian Customs web-site www.carina.hr for information regarding tax refunds on purchases made while in Croatia. The web-site offers information in English. Word to the wise: do not change money with individuals in the streets!

KEY WORDS

bank	**banka** *banka*
cash machine	**bankomat** *bankomat*
cheque	**ček** *chek*
credit card	**kreditna kartica** *kredeetna karteetsa*
exchange office	**mjenjačnica** *myenyachneetsa*
exchange rate	**tečaj** *techay*
money	**novac** *novats*

Where can I change money?	**Gdje mogu promijeniti novac?** *gdye mogoo promeeyeneetee novats*
Where is the nearest cash machine?	**Gdje je najbliži bankomat?** *gdye ye naybleezhee bankomat*

Could you direct me to to the nearest bank/ exchange office?

Možete li me uputiti do najbliže banke/ mjenjačnice? *mozhete lee me oopooteetee do naybleezhe banke/ myenyachneetse*

What is the exchange rate for the ...?

Koliki je tečaj za ...? *koleekee ye techay za*

American dollar

američki dolar *amereechkee dolar*

Australian dollar

australski dolar *aoostralskee dolar*

British pound

britansku funtu *breetanskoo foontoo*

Canadian dollar

kanadski dolar *kanadskee dolar*

Euro

euro *eooro*

How much is your commission?

Kolika je vaša provizija? *koleeka ye vasha proveezeeya*

Can I change $50 US?

Mogu li promijeniti pedeset američkih dolara? *mogoo lee promeeyeneetee pedeset amereechkeeh dolara*

I'd like 100 kuna notes, please.

Molim novčanice od 100 kuna. *moleem novchaneetse od sto koona*

Can you change these traveller's cheques?

Možete li promijeniti ove putničke čekove?
mozhete lee promeeyeneetee ove pootneechke chekove

I'd like to cash this Eurocheque.

Htio/Htjela bih unovčiti ovaj euroček.
hteeo/htyela beeh oonovcheetee ovay eoorochek

Can I get a cash advance with my credit card?

Mogu li dobiti gotovinu sa svoje kreditne kartice?
mogoo lee dobeetee gotoveenu sa svoye kredeetne karteetse

I need to send money to ...

Trebam poslati novac u ... *trebam poslatee novats oo*

Where do I sign?

Gdje da potpišem?
gdye da potpeeshem

Getting around

DIRECTIONS

LOCAL TRANSPORTATION

Whether on foot, by car or local transport, don't hesitate to ask for directions. Croatians are more than happy to help out the 'lost' tourist. There is major construction happening on just about all of Croatia's roads and highways. Be prepared for detours. Traffic jams, long queues of cars and buses, and reduced speeds on highways, streets and roads are common. See **Arrival and Departure** (p. 37) for information about car rentals, coach, rail, and ferry travel. See **Driving Around Croatia** (p. 77) for information about road assistance, vehicle parts and vehicle trouble.

KEY WORDS

city map	**plan grada** *plan gra*da
highway	**autocesta** *a*oototsesta
road map	**autokarta** *a*ootokarta
street	**ulica** *oo*leetsa
Tourist Information Office	**Turističke informacije** too*ree*steechke eenfor*ma*tseeye

Directions   Putokazi

KEY WORDS

at the corner	**na uglu** *na* oo*gloo*
east	**istok** *ee*stok
north	**sjever** *sy*ever
on foot	**pješice** *pye*sheetse
on the left	**lijevo** *lee*yevo
on the right	**desno** *des*no
one way	**jedan smjer** *y*edan *smyer*

south	**jug** *yoog*
straight ahead	**ravno** *ravno*
turn left/right	**skreni lijevo/desno**
	skrenee leeyevo/desno
west	**zapad** *zapad*

Is this the way to ...?

Je li to put prema ...?
ye lee to poot prema

I'm lost.

Izgubio/Izgubila sam se.
eezgoobeeo/eezgoobeela sam se

Can you help me?

Možete li mi pomoći?
mozhete lee mee pomochee

Where is the ... Hotel?

Gdje je hotel ...? *gdye ye hotel*

Excuse me, I can't find ... street.

Oprostite, ne mogu naći ... ulicu. *oprosteete ne mogoo nachee – ooleetsoo*

How can I get to the city centre?

Kako mogu doći u centar grada? *kako mogoo dochee oo tsentar grada*

Could you direct me to the Tourist Information Office?

Možete li me uputiti do ureda za turističke informacije? *mozhete lee me oopooteetee do ooreda za tooreesteechkee eenformatseeye*

Can I park here?

Mogu li parkirati ovdje?
mogoo lee parkeeratee ovdye

Where is the car park?

Gdje je parkiralište?
gdye ye parkeeraleeshte

Is the market round
the corner?

Je li tržnica iza ugla?
ye lee trzhneetsa eeza oogla

I want a road map for this
area.

**Želim autokartu ove
regije.** *zheleem aootokartoo
ove regeeye*

Can you show me the way
on the map?

**Možete li mi pokazati put
na karti?** *mozhete lee mee
pokazatee poot na kartee*

How far is it?

Koliko je to daleko?
koleeko ye to daleko

How do I get to...?

Kako mogu doći do ...?
kako mogoo dochee do

Should I turn left/right?

**Trebam li skrenuti lijevo/
desno?** *trebam lee
skrenootee leeyevo/desno*

Can I get to ...

Mogu li doći do ...
mogoo lee dochee do

  by car?
  on foot?

    autom? *aootom*
    pješice? *pyesheetse*

Local Transportation   Gradski promet

Croatia's major cities and towns such as Zagreb, Osijek, Split and Dubrovnik have public transportation. Both buses and tramways are a convenient way to get around the cities. Tickets can be bought on board or at newspaper and tabacco kiosks. Check with local tram/bus agents for schedules. Taxis are also available in most cities and towns. Fares vary from community to community; however, before entering a taxi, ask for the rates.

KEY WORDS

bus	**autobus** *aootoboos*
taxi	**taksi** *taksee*
ticket	**karta** *karta*
tram	**tramvaj** *tramvay*

Where is the nearest bus/tram stop?	**Gdje je najbliža autobusna/tramvajska stanica?** *gdye ye naybleezha aootoboosna/tramvayska stanica*
Is this the bus/tram to ...?	**Je li ovo autobus/tramvaj za ...?** *ye lee ovo aootoboos/tramvay za*
Where do I transfer for...?	**Gdje se prelazi za...?** *gdye se prelazee za...*

| How much is the bus/tram ticket? | **Koliko košta autobusna/ tramvajska karta?** *koleeko koshta aootoboosna/ tramvayska karta* |

Two tickets, please. **Dvije karte, molim!** *dveeye karte moleem*

I need a taxi at 20 ... street. **Molim taksi u ulicu ... broj 20.** *moleem taksi oo ooleetsoo – broj dvadeset*

Can you call a taxi for me? **Možete li mi pozvati taksi?** *mozhete lee mee pozvatee taksee*

Take me to this address. **Odvezite me na tu adresu!** *odvezeete me na too adresoo*

How much is the fare to ...? **Koliko košta vožnja do ...?** *koleeko koshta vozhnya do*

Please wait here for a few minutes. **Molim vas, pričekajte ovdje nekoliko minuta!** *moleem vas preechekayte ovdye nekoleeko meenoota*

Keep the change. **Zadržite ostatak.** *zadrzheete ostatak*

Driving Around Croatia

VEHICLE PARTS/TROUBLE

Croatia has the same traffic regulations as established in the majority of European countries. Driving is on the right hand side, and road markings and traffic signs are international. Most highways and motor ways have toll charges. As mentioned before, you will undoubtedly face major construction sites, detours and delays as you drive around Croatia. The *Croatian Automobile Club* (**HAK**) provides emergency services to non-members. Telephone booths can be found along main roads and highways. **HAK** provides 24-hour information in Croatian and English. You can get information about road conditions, ferry delays, and telephone numbers of foreign automobile clubs. Dial **987** for road assistance and information. See **Arrival and Departure** (p. 37) for information regarding car rentals, coach, rail and ferry travel. Check the **Getting Around** unit for directions. See **Dictionary** for specific car parts. Remember: don't hurry, drive safely!

Vehicle Parts/Trouble   Automobilski dijelovi/kvarovi

KEY WORDS

diesel	**dizel** *deezel*
mechanic	**mehaničar** *mehaneechar*
petrol (gas)	**benzin** *benzeen*
petrol (gas) station	**benzinska crpka (pumpa)** *benzeenska tsrpka (poompa)*
towing service	**vučna služba** *voochna sloozhba*

Where is the nearest petrol/
gas station?

**Gdje je najbliža
benzinska crpka/pumpa?**
*gdye ye naybleezha
benzeenska tsrpka/poompa*

I need help.
My car has broken down.

**Trebam pomoć.
Auto mi se pokvario.**
*trebam pomoch – aooto mee
se pokvaroo*

Can you tow me to
a mechanic?

**Možete li me odvući do
mehaničara?** *mozhete lee
me odvoochee do
mehaneechara*

Fill it up, please.

Napunite, molim vas!
napooneete, moleem vas

Please check the oil.

Molim vas, provjerite ulje!
moleem vas provyereete oolye

I need an oil change.

Treba promijeniti ulje.
treba promeeyeneetee oolye

I have a flat tire.

Pukla mi je guma.
pookla mee ye gooma

I've locked myself out of
my van.

**Zaključala su se vrata
moga kombija.**
*zaklyoochala soo se vrata
moga kombeeya*

The engine is overheating.

Motor se pregrijao.
motor se pregreeyao

There is something wrong with the brakes.

Nešto nije u redu s kočnicama. *neshto neeye oo redoo s kochneetsama*

Do you have the spare parts for this car?

Imate li rezervne dijelove za ovaj auto? *eemate lee rezervne deeyelove za ovay aooto*

Can you repair it?

Možete li to popraviti? *mozhete lee to popraveetee*

When will it be ready?

Kad će biti gotovo? *kad che beetee gotovo*

Where is the nearest car wash?

Gdje je najbliža autopraonica? *gdye ye naybleezha aootopraoneetsa*

Eating & Drinking

Croatian Cuisine   Hrvatska kuhinja

Croatian cuisine will delight you in its variety and quality. Every region has its specialities, every region has its culinary customs. From the fresh seafood bounty of the Adriatic to the delicate pastries and cakes of the Pannonian valley, visitors can savour dishes, wines and spirits which reflect the richness and diversity of Croatia.

Every region in Croatia produces exceptional red and white wines. Regional spirits such as plum brandy **šljivovica** *shlyeevoveetsa* and Dalmatian herb brandy **travarica** *trava-reetsa* are usually served before a meal. For dessert, you might want to try a glass of **prošek** *proshek*, a sweet wine which nicely compliments Croatian cakes.

Just a sampling of Croatian cuisine…

* Dalmatian prosciutto with olives — **dalmatinski pršut s maslinama** *dalmateenskee prshoot s masleenama*
* Pag chesse — **paški sir** *pashkee seer*
* Octopus salad — **salata od hobotnice** *salata od hobotneetse*
* Shellfish *buzara* — **školjke na buzaru** *shkolyke na boozaroo*
* Cod stew Dalmatian style — **brodet od bakalara** *brodet od bakalara*
* Dalmatian beef with gnocchi — **pašticada s njokima** *pashtitsada s nyokeema*
* Slavonian sausage — **kulen** *koolen*
* Fresh cottage cheese and sour cream — **sir i vrhnje** *seer ee vrhnye*

- *Štrukli* Zagorje style **zagorski štrukli**
  (a well-known dish from *zagorskee shtrooklee*
  the Zagreb area;
  a cottage cheese crêpe)
- Barley and bean soup **ričet** *reechet*
- Cabbage rolls **sarma** *sarma*
  with sauerkraut
- Stuffed peppers **punjene paprike**
  poonyene papreeke
- Lamb on the spit **janjetina na ražnju**
  yanyeteena na razhnyoo
- Suckling pig on the spit **odojak na ražnju** *odoyak*
  na razhnyoo
- Turkey with *mlinci* **purica s mlincima**
  (mlinci are a side dish *pooreetsa s mleentseema*
  prepared from fat-free dough)
- Veal escalope Zagreb style **zagrebački odrezak**
  zagrebachkee odrezak
- Plum dumplings **knedle od šljiva** *knedle od*
  shlyeeva
- Crêpes with walnuts **palačinke s orasima**
  palacheenke s oraseema
- Fritters **fritule** *freetoole*
- Sour cherry strudel **savijača od višanja**
  saveeyacha od veeshanya
- *Samoborske kremšnite* **samoborske kremšnite**
  (a vanilla custard sandwiched *samoborske kremshneete*
  between light pastry)
- Poppy seed roll **makovnjača** *makovnyacha*
- Hazelnut cake **torta od lješnjaka** *torta od*
  lyeshnyaka

Eating out   Jesti vani

For most Croats, eating out is usually a special affair. Lunch
or supper can comprise of a number of courses, depending
on the type of restaurant at which the event is taking place.
The variety of restaurants has greatly expanded over recent
years and so one can choose the traditional home-style meals
of Croatian restaurants or savour Chinese or Italian specialities. Eating on the run, or just satisfying a sudden hunger
pang can be done at many different kinds of eateries: from
the local bakery which offers savory cheese-filled strudel to
the traditional **konoba** *konoba* where one can eat some
cheese and prosciutto and sample a glass of home-made
wine. Many restaurants' menus are written in English. No
matter where you decide to dine, remember this: always be
ready to meet all sorts of surprises; enjoy the good ones,
ignore the bad ones. **Dobar tek!**

KEY WORDS

breakfast	**doručak** *doroochak*
Dalmatian tavern	**konoba** *konoba*
dinner/supper	**večera** *vechera*
fish restaurant	**riblji restoran** *reeblyee restoran*
lunch	**ručak** *roochak*
pub	**pivnica** *peevneetsa*
restaurant	**gostionica** *gosteeoneetsa*/ **restoran** *restoran*
vegetarian restaurant	**vegetarijanski restoran** *vegetareeyanskee restoran*

Before the Meal

Prije obroka

meal	**obrok** *obrok*
reservation	**rezervacija** *rezervatseeya*

Is there a good restaurant nearby?

Ima li dobar restoran u blizini? *eema lee dobar restoran oo bleezeenee*

Do you serve fish?

Poslužujete li ribu? *posloozhooyete lee reeboo*

I need a table for three.

Trebam stol za troje. *trebam stol za troye*

Can we have a table by the window?

Možemo li dobiti stol do prozora? *mozhemo lee dobeetee stol do prozora*

Do you have a non-smoking section?

Imate li prostor za nepušače? *eemate lee prostor za nepooshache*

Are these seats taken?

Jesu li ova mjesta zauzeta? *yesoo lee ova myesta zaoozeta*

Can we join you?

Možemo li vam se pridružiti? *mozhemo lee vam se preedroozheetee*

Is there a cover charge
(for music)?

**Doplaćuje li se za
glazbu?** *doplachooye lee se
za glazboo*

I'd like to make a reservation
for tonight, at eight o'clock.

**Volio/Voljela bih rezervi-
rati stol za večeras, u
osam sati.** *voleeo/volyela
beeh rezerveeratee stol za
vecheras oo osam satee*

During the Meal

Za vrijeme obroka

See **Dictionary** for specific foods, drinks and cooking ter-
minology.

KEY WORDS

menu	**jelovnik** *yelovneek*
waiter/waitress	**konobar/konobarica**
	konobar/konobareetsa
wine list	**vinska karta** *veenska karta*

Can I see the menu, please?

**Mogu li vidjeti jelovnik,
molim?** *mogoo lee veedyetee
yelovneek moleem*

What would you
recommend?

Što biste vi preporučili?
shto beeste vee preporoocheelee

I'm ready to order.

Htio/Htjela bih naručiti.
*hteeo/htyela beeh
naroocheetee*

Can we order a child's portion?

Možemo li dobiti dječju porciju? *mozhemo lee dobeetee dyechyoo portseeyoo*

We'd like to share the pizza.

Voljeli bismo podijeliti pizzu. *volyelee beesmo podeeyeleetee pizzoo*

I'll have the grilled fish without the Swiss chard.

Uzet ću pečenu ribu bez blitve. *oozet choo pechenoo reeboo bez bleetve*

Can I have a glass of juice?

Mogu li dobiti čašu džusa? *mogoo lee dobeetee chashoo joosa*

I'd like a bottle of …

Volio/Voljela bih bocu … *voleeo/volyela beeh botsoo*

We'd like a half litre of your white house wine.

Voljeli bismo pola litre vašega bijelog domaćeg vina. *volyelee beesmo pola leetre vashega beeyelog domacheg veena*

Can I have a pint of draft beer?

Mogu li dobiti kriglu točenog piva? *mogoo lee dobeetee kreegloo tochenog peeva*

Can we have some more bread, please?

Možemo li dobiti još kruha, molim? *mozhemo lee dobeetee josh krooha moleem*

I need another napkin, please.

Molim vas još jednu salvetu! *moleem vas yosh jednu salvetoo*

I'm sorry, but the steak is not well done.

Žao mi je, ali biftek nije dovoljno pečen. *zhao mee ye alee beeftek neeye dovolyno pechen*

The soup is not warm enough.

Juha nije dovoljno topla. *yooha neeye dovolyno topla*

Cheers!

Živjeli! *zheevyelee*

Enjoy your meal!

Dobar tek! *dobar tek*

After the Meal

Nakon objeda

KEY WORDS

bill	**račun** *rachoon*
cash	**gotovina** *gotoveena*
credit card	**kreditna kartica** *kredeetna karteetsa*

The bill, please.

Račun, molim! *rachoon moleem*

Separate bills, please.

Poseban račun za svakoga, molim! *poseban rachoon za svakoga moleem*

Do you accept credit cards?

Primate li kreditne kartice? *preemate lee kredeetne karteetse*

I think there is a mistake on this bill.

Mislim da ste se zabunili u računu. *meesleem da ste se zabooneelee oo rachoonoo*

I'll pay cash.

Platit ću gotovinom. *plateet choo gotoveenom*

Keep the change.

Zadržite ostatak! *zadrzheete ostatak*

It was delicious.

Bilo je divno. *beelo ye deevno*

Cafés and Pastry/Ice-cream Shops

Kavane i slastičarnice

Sitting at a café's outside terrace and sipping a cappuccino or enjoying a local delicacy such as **kremšnite** *kremshneete* in one of the many pastry/ice-cream shops is a must for all tourists in Croatia. No one hurries you, no one bothers you. Just sit and enjoy! Most cafés and pastry shops keep their price lists on the tables.

KEY WORDS

café	**kavana** *kavana*
cake	**kolač** *kolach*

coffee with…	**kava…** *kava*
artificial sweetener	**s natrenom** *s natrenom*
milk	**s mlijekom** *s mleeyekom*
whipped cream	**sa šlagom** *sa shlagom*
ice-cream	**sladoled** *sladoled*
mineral water	**mineralna voda** *meeneralna voda*
pastry & ice-cream shop	**slastičarnica** *slasteecharneetsa*
tea/ice-tea	**čaj/ledeni čaj** *chay/ledenee chay*
with/without ice	**s ledom/bez leda** *s ledom/bez leda*

Where is the nearest café?
Gdje je najbliža kavana?
gdye ye naybleezha kavana

Is this seat taken?
Je li ovo mjesto zauzeto?
ye lee ovo myesto zaoozeto

What ice-cream flavours do you have?
Koje vrste sladoleda imate? *koye vrste sladoleda eemate*

I'd like two scoops of vanilla ice-cream.
Molim dvije kuglice vanilije. *moleem dveeye koogleetse vaneeleeye*

One espresso with milk, please.
Espreso s mlijekom, molim! *espreso s mleeyekom moleem*

Can I have a slice of walnut cake?
Molim kolač od oraha? *moleem kolach od oraha*

The bill, please.
Račun, molim! *rachoon moleem*

Shopping

Most shops and department stores are open from 8:00 or 9:00 a.m. to 7:00 or 8:00 p.m. In some cities and towns, shops and stores close at 2:00 p.m. on Saturdays. Grocery stores and supermarkets open at 7:00 a.m. Mondays to Saturdays. Only certain grocery stores are open Sundays. In resort areas, most shops have longer working hours seven days a week.

KEY WORDS

bakery	**pekarnica** *pekarneetsa*
book shop	**knjižara** *knyeezhara*
butcher	**mesnica** *mesneetsa*
department store	**robna kuća** *robna koocha*
drugstore	**drogerija** *drogereeya*
flower shop	**cvjećarnica** *tsvyecharneetsa*
grocery store	**prodavaonica živežnih namirnica** *prodavaoneetsa zheevezhneeh nameerneetsa*
jeweller	**zlatar** *zlatar*
market	**tržnica** *trzhneetsa*
news stand	**prodavaonica novina** *prodavaoneetsa noveena*
shop/store	**prodavaonica** *prodavaoneetsa*, **dućan** *doochan*
tobacconist	**trafikant** *trafeekant*

General information

Opće obavijesti

Where can I get …?

Gdje mogu dobiti …?
gdye mogoo dobeetee

Where can I find …?	**Gdje mogu naći …?**
	gdye mogoo nachee
Is there a … near here?	**Nalazi li se u blizini …?**
	nalazee lee se oo bleezeenee
Is it open now?	**Je li sada otvoreno?**
	ye lee sada otvoreno
Can you show me the way to the …please?	**Možete li mi pokazati put do …?** *mozhete lee mee pokazatee poot do*
Do you have/sell …?	**Imate li/Prodajete li …?**
	eemate lee/prodayete lee
I'm looking for …	**Tražim …** *trazheem*
I'd like to buy …	**Htio/Htjela bih kupiti …**
	hteeo/htyela beeh koopeetee
I need a/some …	**Trebam/Trebaju mi …**
	trebam/trebayoo mee

Self-service/ Grocery store	**Samoposluživanje/ Prodavaonica živežnih namirnica**

The prices for unpacked food items are given in kilograms. Delicatessen goods are priced in kilograms but are sold in grams or in decagrams. See **Dictionary** for specific food items.

I'd like 200 grams/20 decagrams of …

Želio /Željela bih dvjesto grama/dvadeset deka… *zheleeo/zhelyela beeh dvyesto grama/dvadeset deka*

cheese
ham
salami

sira *seera*
šunke *shoonke*
salame *salame*

Could you give me half of this bread, please?

Molim polovicu ovoga kruha! *moleem poloveetsoo ovoga krooha*

Do you have low-fat yoghurt?

Imate li jogurt s malo masnoće? *eemate lee yogurt s malo masnoche*

Two pairs of Frankfurters, please.

Dva para hrenovki, molim! *dva para hrenovkee moleem.*

Please give me a piece of this salami.

Dajte mi, molim, komadić ove salame. *dayte mee moleem komadeech ove salame*

A little more/less, please.

Malo više/manje, molim. *malo veeshe/manye moleem*

Sliced, please.

Narezano, molim. *narezano moleem*

Where are biscuits?

Gdje su keksi? *gdye soo keksee*

I need a small box of detergent.	**Molim vas malu kutiju deterdženta!** *moleem vas maloo kooteeyoo deterjenta*
A bottle of non-carbonated water, please.	**Bocu negazirane vode, molim!** *botsoo negazeerane vode moleem*
The shelf life has expired.	**Rok upotrebe je prošao.** *rok upotrebe ye proshao*

At the Farmers' Market   Na tržnici

In cities and towns, food products are sold at open-air farmers' markets which are open from 7:00 a.m. to about 3:00 p.m. every day. You can buy local and imported fruits, vegetables, dairy products, eggs and flowers. At some markets even fresh meat and fish are sold. See **Dictionary** for specific food items.

I'd like a kilo of … please.	**Molim vas kilu …** *moleem vas keeloo*
apples	**jabuka** *yabooka*
pears	**krušaka** *krooshaka*
plums	**šljiva** *shlyeeva*
Can I have half a kilo of …?	**Mogu li dobiti pola kile …?** *mogoo lee dobeetee pola keele*
beans	**mahuna** *mahoona*
carrots	**mrkve** *mrkve*
tomatoes	**rajčica** *raycheetsa/* **paradajza** *paradayza*

Give me the ones over there, please.

Dajte mi one tamo, molim! *dayte mee one tamo moleem*

How much are the …?

Koliko koštaju …? *koleeko koshtayoo*

melons
nectarines
peppers

dinje *deenye*
nektarine *nektareene*
paprike *papreeke*

Thanks. I don't want them.

Hvala, ne trebaju mi. *hvala ne trebayoo mee*

It isn't fresh/ripe.

Nije svježe/zrelo. *neeye svyezhe/zrelo*

They aren't fresh/ripe.

Nisu svježe/zrele. *neesoo svyezhe/zrele*

It's too expensive.

Preskupo je. *preskoopo ye*

I don't understand how much it is.

Ne razumijem koliko to košta. *ne razoomeeyem koleeko to koshta*

Write it down, please.

Molim, napišite mi iznos! *moleem napeesheete mee eeznos*

Souvenir/Gift Shop   Suveniri/Darovi

There are many shops, kiosks and stands, especially in resort areas, where you can buy souvenirs and gifts for family and friends. The exquisite hand-woven lace from the island of Pag, a silk man's tie **kravata** *kravata* which, by the way, is a Croatian 'invention', crystal wine glasses from Samobor, or a bottle of olive oil from the island of Korčula are but a few products Croatia has to offer. Enjoy your shopping!

KEY WORDS

genuine	**pravi** *pravee*
	nije imitacija
	neeye eemeetatseeya
handicraft	**ručno izrađeno**
	roochno eezrajeno
hand-made	**ručni rad** *roochnee rad*

I'd like to buy a souvenir from this region.
Želio bih kupiti suvenir iz ovog kraja. *zheleeo beeh koopeetee suveneer eez ovog kraya*

What would you suggest as a gift for my
Što biste sugerirali kao dar za ...? *shto beeste soogereeralee kao dar za*

daughter/wife
moju kćerku/ženu *moyoo kcherkoo/zhenoo*

son/husband
moga sina/muža *moga seena/moozha*

Would you show me some silver ..., please?

Molim vas pokažite mi srebrne ... *moleem vas pokazheete mee srebrne*

earrings
bracelets
rings
necklaces

    naušnice *naooshneetse*
    narukvice *narookveetse*
    prstene *prstene*
    ogrlice *ogrleetse*

Do you have any ... made of stone?

Imate li ... izrađene od kamena? *eemate lee – eezrajene od kamena*

candlesticks
vases
bowles

    svijećnjake *sveeyechnyake*
    vaze *vaze*
    zdjele *zdyele*

That's too expensive.

To je preskupo. *to ye preskoopo*

I'd like something less expensive.

Volio/Voljela bih nešto jeftinije. *voleeo/volyela beeh neshto yefteeneeye*

Please show me those...things.

Pokažite mi one stvari od... *pokazheete mee one stvaree od*

copper
wooden
crystal

    bakra *bakra*
    drveta *drveta*
    kristala *kreestala*

Could I see the little ceramic houses?

Mogu li vidjeti te male keramičke kućice? *mogoo lee veedyetee te male kerameechke koocheetse*

I'm looking for embroidered table linen.	**Tražim izvezene stolnjake i salvete.** *trazheem eez-vezene stolnyake ee salvete*
I'd like a …doily.	**Htio/Htjela bih … milje/podložak.** *hteeo/htyela beeh – meelye/podlozhak*
crochet	**kačkani/heklani** *kachkanee/heklanee*
lace	**čipke** *cheepke*
Do you have a recent CD with …?	**Imate li najnoviji CD …?** *eemate lee naynoveeyee ce de*
Dalmatian songs	**s dalmatinskim pjesmama** *s dalmateenskeem pyesmama*
Croatian pop music	**s hrvatskim hitovima** *s hrvatskeem heetoveema*
Wrap it up well, please!	**Dobro mi to zamotajte, molim!** *dobro mee to zamotayte moleem*

Clothing and shoes   Odjeća i obuća

Many boutiques and stores carry both imported and locally produced clothes and shoes. It is possible to exchange the items you have bought if you have a receipt. In most stores you cannot get a cash refund for the item you want to return; you can only exchange it for another item. See the **Dictionary** for specific items. The sizes are continental and differ from British and American sizes. The following tables will help you find your continental sizes.

Men's Suits and Coats

UK	34	36	38
USA	44	46	48
CRO	44	46	48

Men's Pants/Trousers

UK	46	48	50
USA	32	34	36
CRO	46	48	50

Women's Dresses, Skirts, Blouses, Suits

UK	10	12	14
USA	6	8	10
CRO	36	38	40

Men's Shirts (Neck Size)

UK	15	$15^{1/2}$	16
USA	15	$15^{1/2}$	16
CRO	38	40	42

Women's Shoes

UK	4	5	6
USA	6	7	8
CRO	36	37	38

Men's Shoes

UK	7	8	9
USA	9-$9^{1/2}$	10-$10^{1/2}$	11-$11^{1/2}$
CRO	42	43	44

I'm just looking.

Samo razgledavam.
samo razgledavam

I'm looking for a summer dress.

Tražim ljetnu haljinu.
trazheem lyetnoo halyeenoo

Do you have any linen blouses?

Imate li lanene bluze?
eemate lee lanene blooze

I'd like a silk top.

Htjela bih svilenu bluzu bez rukava. *htyela beeh sveelenoo bloozoo bez rookava*

I need a cotton shirt.

Trebam pamučnu košulju.
trebam pamoochnoo koshoolyoo

Do you have it in other colours?

Imate li to u drugim bojama? *eemate lee to oo droogeem boyama*

I'm size 42.

Nosim broj četrdeset dva. *noseem broy chetrdeset dva*

Can I try it on?

Mogu li to isprobati? *mogoo lee to eesprobatee*

Where is the change room?

Gdje je kabina? *gdye ye kabeena*

It's too small/big.

Premalo/Preveliko je. *premalo/preveleeko ye*

Do you have white trousers in my size?

Imate li moj broj bijelih hlača? *eemate lee moy broy beeyeleeh hlacha*

They don't fit me.

Ne pristaju mi. *ne preestayoo mee*

They're too long/short.

Preduge/Prekratke su. *predooge/prekratke soo*

I'd like a woolen pullover.

Htio/Htjela bih vuneni pulover. *hteeo/htyela beeh voonenee poolover*

I'll take it.

Uzet ću to. *oozet choo to*

Do you have it in a bigger/ smaller size?

Imate li veći/manji broj? *eemate lee vechee/manyee broy*

Can you show me some swimsuits/trunks?	**Možete li mi pokazati kupaće kostime/gaće?** *mozhete lee mee pokazatee koopache kosteeme/gache*
I want a pair of sandals.	**Molim vas sandale!** *moleem vas sandale*
I need size 39.	**Trebam broj trideset devet.** *trebam broy treedeset devet*
I'd like the brown ones.	**Želim ih u smeđoj boji.** *zheleem eeh oo smejoy boyee*
Please show me the black boots with the high/low heel.	**Pokažite mi crne čizme s niskom/visokom petom.** *pokazheete mee tsrne cheezme s neeskom/veesokom petom*
Are they waterproof?	**Jesu li otporne na vlagu?** *yesoo lee otporne na vlagoo*
Can I exchange it?	**Mogu li to zamijeniti?** *mogoo lee to zameeyeneetee*
I'll pay cash/by credit card.	**Platit ću gotovinom/ kreditnom karticom.** *plateet choo gotoveenom/ kredeetnom karteetsom*

Services

AT THE HAIRDRESSER'S/
HAIR STYLIST'S/
BARBER SHOP

AT THE WATCHMAKER'S

AT THE PHOTOGRAPHER'S

You can find hair salons for men and women in all cities, towns, resort areas as well as in big hotels. Most are open from 8:00 a.m. to 8:00 p.m. Some close during the day, so check their working hours before you go. It is better to make an appointment; otherwise, be prepared to sit and wait for quite a while.

KEY WORDS

barber shop	**brijačnica** *bree*yachneetsa
cut	**šišanje** *shee*shanye
hair	**kosa** *ko*sa
hairdresser saloon	**frizerski salon** *freezerskee salon*
wash	**pranje** *pran*ye

I'd like to make an appointment.	**Htjela bih se naručiti.** *htye*la beeh se naroo*chee*tee
At what time are you open?	**Kad ste otvoreni?** *kad* ste *otvorenee*
When can I come?	**Kad mogu doći?** *kad mo*goo *do*chee
A shampoo and set, please.	**Pranje i frizuru molim!** *pra*nye ee free*zoo*roo *mo*leem

I'd like a cut and blow-dry.	**Želim šišanje i feniranje.** *zheleem sheeshanye ee feneeranye*
Not too short, please.	**Ne prekratko, molim!** *ne prekratko moleem*
A little bit shorter.	**Malo kraće.** *malo krache*
Could you colour my hair?	**Želim farbanje.** *zheleem farbanye*
Dark blond, please.	**Tamnije plavu, molim.** *tamneeye plavoo moleem*
I'd like to highlight my hair.	**Želim pramenove.** *zheleem pramenove*
A little/no hairspray, please.	**Malo/Bez laka za kosu, molim!** *malo/bez laka za kosu moleem*

At the Watchmaker's   Kod urara

alarm clock	**budilica** *boodeeleetsa*
battery	**baterija** *batereeya*
repair (v)	**popraviti** *popraveetee*
watch	**sat** *sat*

| My watch has stopped. Could you have a look at it? | **Stao mi je sat.** **Možete li ga pogledati?** *stao mee ye sat* *mozhete lee ga pogledatee* |

| Is the battery dead? | **Je li se baterija istrošila?** *ye lee se batereeya eestrosheela* |

| Could you replace the battery? | **Možete li promijeniti bateriju?** *mozhete lee promeeyeneetee batereeyoo* |

| I need a new band for this watch. | **Trebam novi remen za sat.** *trebam novee remen za sat* |

| Something is wrong with this alarm clock. Could you see to it? | **Nešto nije u redu s ovom budilicom. Možete li je pogledati?** *neshto neeye oo redoo s ovom boodeeleetsom mozhete lee ye pogledatee* |

At the Photographer's   Kod fotografa

camera	**fotoaparat** *fotoaparat*
photo	**fotografija** *fotografeeya*
take photos	**fotografirati** *fotografeeratee*

Would you take the film out of the camera and develop it?

Možete li izvaditi film iz aparata i razviti ga? *mozhete lee eezvadeetee feelm eez aparata ee razveetee ga*

When will the photos be ready?

Kada će slike biti gotove? *kada che sleeke beetee gotove*

I need a roll of colour film with 36 exposures.

Trebam film u boji sa 36 slika. *trebam feelm u boyee s treedeset shest sleeka*

Could you put the film in the camera?

Možete li staviti film u aparat? *mozhete lee staveetee film oo aparat*

Something is wrong with my camera.
Could you repair it?

Nešto nije u redu s mojim aparatom. Možete li ga popraviti? *neshto neeye oo redoo s moyeem aparatom – mozhete lee ga popraveetee*

KEY WORDS

contact lenses	**kontaktne leće** *kontaktne leche*
frame	**okvir** *okveer*
glasses	**naočale** *naochale*
sunglasses	**sunčane naočale** *soonchane naochale*

Can you help me?

Možete li mi pomoći?
mozhete lee mee pomochee

One of the lenses has fallen out. Could you fix it?

Jedno je staklo ispalo. Možete li to popraviti?
yedno ye staklo eespalo mozhete lee to popraveetee

Can you fix the handle, please?

Možete li, molim vas, učvrstiti dršku? *mozhete lee moleem vas uchvrsteetee drshkoo*

Do you have preserving solution for contact lenses?

Imate li tekućinu za čuvanje leća? *eemate lee tekoocheenoo za choovanye lecha*

Postal and Telecommunication Services

AT THE POST OFFICE
INTERNET SERVICES

TELEPHONING

Post offices can be easily found by their logo **HP** (**Hrvatska pošta** *hrvatska poshta*) or by a bright yellow sign showing a black postal horn. In cities, towns and tourist resorts post offices are open from 7:00 a.m. to 7:00 p.m. You can buy stamps and postcards, send faxes or telegrams, and make long-distance and international calls at the post office. In some resorts you can even change money there. As the postage for international mail varies depending on destination, it is best to send your international mail from the post office. Stamps can be bought at the post office and at some news stands; postcards are sold at many kiosks and stands.

KEY WORDS

airmail	**avionom** *aveeonom*
envelope	**koverta** *koverta*
letter	**pismo** *peesmo*
postage	**poštarina** *poshtareena*
postcard	**razglednica** *razgledneetsa*
post office	**pošta** *poshta*
stamp	**marka** *marka*

I need some stamps.

Trebam marke!
trebam marke

Where can I buy stamps?

Gdje mogu kupiti marke?
gdye mogoo koopeetee marke

Where's the post office?

Gdje je pošta?
gdye ye poshta

What time does the post office open/close?	**U koliko se sati otvara/zatvara pošta?** *oo koleeko se satee otvara/zatvara poshta*
I'd like to send these postcards to ...	**Htio/Htjela bih poslati ove razglednice u ...** *hteeo/htyela bih poslatee ove razgledneetse oo*
Great Britain	**Veliku Britaniju** *veleekoo breetaneeyoo*
United States	**Sjedinjene Američke Države** *syedeenyene amereechke drzhave*
Canada	**Kanadu** *kanadoo*
Australia	**Australiju** *australeeyoo*
How much is the stamp for this postcard?	**Koliko stoji marka za razglednicu?** *koleeko stoyee marka za razgledneetsoo*
What is the postage on ... letter?	**Kolika je poštarina za ... pismo?** *koleeka ye poshtareena za – peesmo*
a registered	**preporučeno** *preporoocheno*
an express	**hitno** *heetno*
a regular	**obično** *obeechno*
Send this by airmail, please.	**Molim pošaljite to avionom!** *moleem poshalyeete to aveeonom*

Which counter is for sending telegrams?	**S kojeg se šaltera šalju brzojavi?** *s koyeg se shaltera shalyoo brzojavee*
How much is it per word?	**Koliko stoji jedna riječ?** *koleeko stoyee yedna reeyech*
Could you help me fill out this form?	**Možete li mi pomoći ispuniti ovaj formular?** *mozhete lee mee pomochee eespooneetee ovay formoolar*
I'd like to send this message by fax.	**Želim poslati poruku faksom.** *zheleem poslatee porookoo faksom*
How much will this telefax cost?	**Koliko će koštati ovaj telefaks?** *koleeko che koshtatee ovay telefaks*

Internet Services · Usluge interneta

If you are looking for Internet services you can check with the hotel receptionist where to get them. Another possibility is to check www.netcafeguide.com before you go on holidays. This site lists locations in 151 countries. Many Internet cafés have been opened in larger cities and resort areas across Croatia.

Is it possible to get Internet access from here?	**Mogu li se odavde priključiti na Internet?** *mogoo lee se odavde preeklyoocheetee na internet*

Could I send an e-mail message from your computer?	**Mogu li poslati e-mail poruku s vašeg kompjutora?** *mogoo lee poslatee e-mail porookoo s vasheg kompyootora*
How much do you charge per minute?	**Koliko košta jedna minuta?** *koleeko koshta yedna meenoota*
Can someone send me an e-mail to your address?	**Mogu li primati e-mail na vašu adresu?** *mogoo lee preematee e-mail na vashoo adresoo*
What is your e-mail address?	**Koja je vaša e-mail adresa?** *koya ye vasha e-mail adresa*
Show me how to log on, please.	**Molim vas, pokažite mi kako se uključujem.** *moleem vas pokazheete mee kako se uklyoochooyem*

Telephoning   Telefoniranje

In Croatia, you can find public telephone booths everywhere; however, you will need a telephone card. Cards can be bought at the post office, at tobacco shops called **DUHAN** and at news stands called **TISAK**. Local, long distance and international calls can be made from public telephone booths. You can use your cellular phone to make local, long distance and international calls, using local **GSM** operators: **HTnet** and **VIPnet**.

If you want to make a long distance or international call, you have to buy a card with a minimum of 100 impulses. To call another country, dial 00, wait for a dial tone, and then dial the country code, followed by the area code, and finally the number you wish to reach. Diagrams above the telephone in the booth will direct you on how to operate the phone.

To make a collect call, dial the operator at **901**. Tell her/him the number of the person you wish to reach. After the call has been accepted, the operator will put you through. An easier way is to go the nearest post office and make the call from there.

If the person you want to reach leaves a message on the answering machine, you will usually hear the following: **Dobili ste broj ... Nakon zvučnog signala ostavite poruku i broj telefona na koji vas možemo nazvati.** *You have reached ... After the tone, leave a message and the number at which you can be reached.*

See **Useful Telephone Numbers** for various services provided by **HT** (Croatian Telecommunication). Word to the wise: it is cheaper to use public telephones than making the call from your hotel. Also, international calls are less costly when made in the evening and early morning (7:00 p.m. to 7:00 a.m.).

international call	**inozemni razgovor**
	eenozemnee razgovor
make a collect call	**razgovor plativ u dolasku**
	razgovor plateev oo dolaskoo
make a phone call	**telefonirati** *telefoneeratee*
operator	**telefonist na centrali**
	telefoneest na tsentralee
telephone	**telefon** *telefon*
telephone booth	**telefonska govornica**
	telefonska govorneetsa
telephone card	**telefonska kartica**
	telefonska karteetsa

Where is the nearest
telephone booth?

**Gdje je najbliža
telefonska govornica?**
*gdye ye naybleezha
telefonska govorneetsa*

Where can I buy
a telephone card?

**Gdje mogu kupiti
telefonsku karticu?** *gdye
mogoo koopeetee telefonskoo
karteetsoo*

Excuse me, could you show
me how to use
the telephone card, please?

**Oprostite, možete mi
pokazati kako se rabi
telefonska kartica?**
*oprosteete mozhete mee
pokazatee kako se rabee
telefonska karteetsa*

Can I get the phone directory, please?

Molim vas telefonski imenik! *moleem vas telefonskee eemeneek*

I want to make an international call.

Želim nazvati inozemstvo. *zheleem nazvatee eenozemstvo*

How do I call the operator?

Kako mogu dobiti centralu? *kako mogoo dobeetee tsentraloo*

Could you give me the number of Mr/Mrs ... . His/her address is ...

Mogu li dobiti broj gospodina/ gospode ... Njegova/Njezina adresa jest ... *mogoo lee dobeetee broy gospodeena/gospoje nyegova/nyezeena adresa yest*

Ann Peters speaking.

Na telefonu je Ann Peters. *na telefonoo je Ann Peters*

Can I speak to Mr/Mrs ..., please?

Mogu li razgovarati s gospodinom/gospodom ...? *mogoo lee razgovaratee s gospodeenom/s gospojom*

Speak more slowly, please.

Molim vas, govorite sporije! *moleem vas govoreete sporeeye*

When is he/she at home in the evening?	**Kad će biti večeras kod kuće?** *kad che beetee vecheras kod kooche*
Could you repeat that, please?	**Možete li to ponoviti?** *mozhete lee to ponoveetee*
Sorry, you got the wrong number.	**Žao mi je, pogrešan broj.** *zhao mee ye pogreshan broy*
She/he could reach me at 258-7496 in the evening.	**Može me dobiti navečer na broju 258-7496.** *mozhe me dobeetee navecher na broyoo dva pet osam sedam cheteeree devet shest*
Could I leave a message?	**Mogu li ostaviti poruku?** *mogoo lee ostaveetee porookoo*
Tell him/her to call me back.	**Recite mu/joj da me nazove.** *retseete moo/yoy da me nazove*

Sports, Leisure & Entertainment

AT THE BEACH/AT THE POOL

LEISURE AND ENTERTAINMENT

SPORTS AND RECREATION

One of the best places to get information regarding local concerts, sports tournaments, recreational activities or cultural events is at the local Tourist Information Bureau. Hotels provide information as well. Check also **At the Tourist Office**. See **Dictionary** for specific sports and activities.

At the Beach/At the Pool   Na plaži/bazenu

KEY WORDS

beach	**plaža** *plazha*
sunscreen lotion	**losion za sunčanje** *loseeon za soonchanye*
swimming pool	**bazen** *bazen*
towel	**ručnik** *roochneek*

Is the beach far from here?	**Je li plaža daleko odavde?** *ye lee plazha daleko odavde*
Is it a sandy beach?	**Je li to pješčana plaža?** *ye lee to pyeshchana plazha*
Are there swimming lessons for children?	**Ima li škola plivanja za djecu?** *eema lee shkola pleevanja za dyetsoo*
Is there a lifeguard?	**Ima li spasilaca?** *eema lee spaseelatsa*
How much do you charge for…?	**Koliko naplaćujete za…?** *koleeko naplachooyete za*
a deck chair	**ležaljku** *lezhalykoo*
a parasol	**suncobran** *soontsobran*

Is there an entrance fee?	**Moramo li platiti ulaznicu?** *moramo lee plateetee oolazneetsoo*
Where can I rent a boat?	**Gdje mogu unajmiti čamac?** *gdye mogoo oonaymeetee chamats*
I want to water ski.	**Želim skijati na vodi.** *zheleem skeeyatee na vodee*
Is there beach volleyball?	**Može li se na plaži igrati odbojka na pijesku?** *mozhe lee se na plazhee eegratee odboyka na peeyeskoo*

Leisure and Entertainment

Slobodno vrijeme i zabava

The Tourist Information Bureau will have a list of all concerts, theatre productions and festivals. The TIB has information regarding local museums, galleries and places of interest. Local newspapers will also advertise special events. All foreign movies in Croatia, both on television and in theatres, are shown in their original language with Croatian subtitles. Check the local newspapers for what's playing where. See **At the Tourist Office** for more information.

KEY WORDS

concert	**koncert** *kontsert*
disco	**diskoteka** *deeskoteka*

movie theatre	**kino** *keeno*
museum	**muzej** *moozey*
theatre	**kazalište** *kazaleeshte*
tickets	**ulaznice** *oolazneetse*

What are the gallery's working hours?

Kada radi galerija? *kada radee galereeya*

Where's the movie theatre?

Gdje je kino? *gdye ye keeno*

Can you recommend something for children?

Možete li preporučiti nešto za djecu? *mozhete lee preporoocheetee neshto za dyetsoo*

Are there guided tours in English?

Imate li vodiča koji govori engleski? *eematee lee vodeecha koyee govoree engleskee*

What is there to do this evening?

Što možemo raditi večeras? *shto mozhemo radeetee vecheras*

Where can I buy tickets for...?

Gdje mogu kupiti ulaznice za...? *gdye mogoo koopeetee oolazneetse za*

Can I reserve two tickets for...?

Mogu li rezervirati dvije ulaznice za...? *mogoo lee rezerveeratee dveeye oolazneetse za*

When does the concert begin?	**Kad počinje koncert?** *kad pocheenye kontsert*
Is there live entertainment at...?	**Imate li živu glazbu u ...?** *eemate lee zheevoo glazboo oo*
Are there discos/night-clubs?	**Ima li ovdje disko/noćnih klubova?** *eema lee ovdye deesko/nochneeh kloobova*

Sports and Recreation   Sportovi

There are many sports and recreational activities organised throughout Croatia: from sky-diving to wild river rafting to horseback riding. Again, your best bet to get information about local centres, activities and events is at the Tourist Information Bureau or at your hotel.

KEY WORDS

fitness centre/ health club	**fitnes centar** *feetnes tsentar*
sports	**sportovi** *sportovee*

Where is the nearest sporting goods store?	**Gdje je najbliža prodavaonica sportske opreme?** *gdye ye naybleezha prodavaoneetsa sportske opreme*
Where can I play tennis?	**Gdje mogu igrati tenis?** *gdye mogoo eegratee tenees*

Is there a fitness club?

Gdje je fitnes centar?
gdye ye feetnes tsentar

I want to rent a bicycle.

Htio/Htjela bih unajmiti bicikl. *hteeo/htyela beeh oonaymeetee beetseekl*

Are there scuba diving courses here?

Imate li školu ronjenja na bocu/kisik? *eemate lee shkoloo ronyenya na botsoo/keeseek*

How much does it cost per hour?

Koliko košta po satu?
koleeko koshta po satoo

Do you rent equipment?

Iznajmljujete li opremu?
eeznaymlyooyete lee opremoo

Is there a football game this evening?

Igra li se večeras nogometna utakmica? *eegra lee se vecheras nogometna ootakmeetsa*

Where can I play volleyball?

Gdje mogu igrati odbojku?
gdye mogoo eegratee odboykoo

Health Care & Emergencies

N AN EMERGENCY

WITH A DOCTOR/NURSE
AT THE DENTIST'S

AT THE PHARMACY

Health care in Croatia is good. Although not all the facilities are modernised, the medical staff is highly trained and qualified. A great number of doctors speak English. When travelling anywhere abroad, always be prepared. Contact your local health insurance company before arriving in Croatia for details about your coverage. If you receive treatment in a public hospital or clinic in Croatia, you will receive a bill. There are local public health centres throughout Croatia. In an emergency, this would be the first place you would go to as there is medical staff on duty 24 hours a day. Call **988** (Directory Assistance) to get the telephone number of your nearest public health centre. See **Dictionary** for specific ailments and parts of body.

KEY WORDS

ambulance	**kola hitne pomoći**
	kola heetne pomochee
doctor	**doktor** *doktor*
first aid	**prva pomoć** *prva pomoch*
hospital	**bolnica** *bolneetsa*
public health centre	**dom zdravlja** *dom zdravlya*

In an Emergency   Hitna pomoć

- To call an ambulance, dial 94.
- To call the police, dial 92.
- To call the fire department, dial 93.
- To call the public emergency centre, dial 985.
- To call road assistance, dial 987.

Where is the nearest hospital?

Gdje je najbliža bolnica?
gdye ye **nay**bleezha
bolneetsa

Immediately send the
ambulance!

**Odmah pošaljite kola
hitne pomoći!** *odmah*
*po*shalyeete *kola heet*ne
*po*mochee

Please call the police.

**Molim vas pozovite
policiju.** *moleem vas*
po*zo*veete po*lee*tseeyoo

There's been
an accident at …

Dogodila se nezgoda na…
*do*go*deela se* **nez**goda *na*

There is a fire at …

Požar je u … *pozhar* ye *oo*

I've been robbed.

Okraden sam.
o*kra*den *sam*

I need help.
I'm at …

**Trebam pomoć.
Ja sam na/u …** *trebam*
pomoch – **ya** *sam* na*loo*

I need an ambulance at …

**Trebam kola hitne
pomoći u…** *trebam* **kola**
heetne **po**mochee *oo*

I need a doctor.

Trebam doktora.
trebam **dok**tora

Thank you for your help.

Hvala vam na pomoći.
*hva*la *vam na* **po**mochee

With a Doctor/Nurse

S doktorom/ medicinskom sestrom

KEY WORDS

doctor's office	**ordinacija** *ordeenatseeya*
medication	**lijek** *leeyek*
nurse	**medicinska sestra** *medeetseenska sestra*

This hurts.	**Ovo boli.** *ovo bolee*
I'm allergic to penicillin.	**Alergičan sam na penicilin.** *alergeechan sam na peneetseeleen*
My child had a severe fall.	**Moje je dijete palo.** *moye ye deeyete palo*
My friend has cut himself severely.	**Moj se prijatelj opasno porezao.** *moy se preeyately opasno porezao*
My husband has a high temperature.	**Moj muž ima visoku temperaturu.** *moy moozh eema veesokoo temperatooroo*
I've twisted my ankle.	**Uganuo/la sam gležanj.** *ooganooo/la sam glezhany*
I think I've broken my arm.	**Mislim da sam slomio/la ruku.** *meesleem da sam slomeeo/la rookoo*

I have a severe headache.

Imam jaku glavobolju.
eemam yakoo glavobolyoo

I can't move my right hand.

Ne mogu micati desnom rukom. *ne mogoo meetsatee desnom rookom*

He's been unconscious for over a minute.

Bio je u nesvijesti više od jedne minute. *beeo ye oo nesveeyestee veeshe od yedne meenoote*

Do I need stitches?

Morate li me šivati?
morate lee me sheevatee

Do I need an x-ray?

Trebam li rentgenski pregled? *trebam lee rentgenskee pregled*

Do I need a prescription?

Trebam li recept?
trebam lee retsept

At the Dentist's

Kod zubara

KEY WORDS

dentist	**zubar/zubarica** *zoobar/zoobareetsa*
tooth/teeth	**zub/zubi** *zoob/zoobee*

I have a severe toothache.

Imam jaku zubobolju.
eemam yakoo zoobobolyoo

My child has chipped a tooth.

Moje je dijete slomilo zub.
moye ye deeyete slomeelo zoob

My denture is broken.	**Slomila mi se proteza.** *slomeela mee se proteza*

At the Pharmacy — U ljekarni

Pharmacies in Croatia not only fill prescriptions, but also sell such items as over the counter medication, medical supplies, cosmetics and vitamins. A pharmacy's symbol is the flashing green cross.

KEY WORDS

pharmacist	**farmaceut** *farmatseoot*
pharmacy	**ljekarna** *lyekarna*
prescription	**recept** *retsept*

What kind of pain relievers do you have?	**Što imate protiv bolova?** *shto eemate proteev bolova*
What do you recommend for a sunburn?	**Što preporučujete za opekline od sunca?** *shto preporoochooyete za opekleene od soontsa*
I need bandages.	**Trebaju mi flasteri.** *trebayoo mee flasteree*
Can you fill this prescription?	**Možete li mi izdati lijek po ovom receptu?** *mozhete lee mee eezdatee leeyek po ovom retseptoo*

Embassies

There are situations when you will need the assistance of your Embassy. Below is the list of Embassies in Croatia. If your country's Embassy is not listed below, your Embassy is then probably situated in Vienna, Austria. Call **902** (**International Directory Inquiries**) for the number.
Dial the 01 prefix before the number if you are calling from outside Zagreb.

The telephone numbers might be changed. Directory Assistance (988) will provide you with new numbers.

Albania 481-0679
Australia, Nova Ves 11, Zagreb 489-1200
Austria 488-1050
Belgium. 457-8901
Bosnia & Herzegovina 468-3761
Bulgaria 482-3336
Canada, Prilaz Gjure Deželića 4, Zagreb 488-1200
Chile 461-1958
China 463-7011
Czech Republic 617-7246
Egypt. 483-4272
Finland 481-1662
France. 489-3600
Germany 615-8105
Greece. 481-0444
Guinea-Bissau 466-3500
Hungary 489-0900
India 487-3241
Iran. 457-8983
Italy. 484-6386
Japan. 467-7755
Malaysia 483-4347

Netherlands 468-4880
Norway 492-2829
Poland 489-9444
Portugal 488-2210
Republic of Macedonia 492-2903
Romania 467-7550
Russian Federation 375-5038
Serbia and Montenegro 457-9067
Slovakia 484-8941
Slovenia 631-1000
Spain 484-8950
Sweden 492-5100
Switzerland 487-8800
Turkey 485-5200
Ukraine 461-6296
United Kingdom, I. Lučića 4, Zagreb 600-9100
United States of America,
   Ulica Thomasa Jeffersona 2, Zagreb 661-2200
Vatican City 467-3995

A

able sposoban *sposoban*

about o *o*, otprilike *otpreeleeke*
  it's about him radi se o
  njemu *radee se o nyemoo*
  it's about 10 miles to je
  otprilike 10 milja *to ye
  otpreeleeke deset meelya*

above iznad *eeznad*, nad *nad*

abroad u inozemstvu
  oo eenozemstvoo

absent odsutan *odsootan*

accept (v) prihvatiti
  preehvateetee, primiti
  preemeetee

accident nezgoda *nezgoda*,
  nesreća *nesrecha*

accommodation smještaj
  smyeshtay

across preko *preko*, s one
  strane *s one strane*

action akcija *aktseeya*;
  postupak *postoopak*

activity aktivnost
  akteevnost

actual sadašnji *sadashnyee*;
  stvarni *stvarnee*

add (v) dodati *dodatee*

additional dodatan
  dodatan

address adresa *adresa*

admire (v) diviti se
  deeveetee se

administration admini-
  stracija *admeeneestratseeya*,
  uprava *ooprava*

admission ulaznina
  oolazneena
  free admission slobodan
  ulaz *slobodan oolaz*

Adriatic Jadransko more
  yadransko more

adult odrasla osoba *odrasla
  osoba*

advantage prednost *prednost*

adventure avantura
  avantoora

advice savjet *savyet*

aerobic aerobika *aerobeeka*

afford (v) priuštiti (si)
  preeooshteetee (see)

afraid prestrašen *prestrashen*,
  uplašen *ooplashen*
  I'm afraid bojim se *boyeem se*

after nakon *nakon*; iza *eeza*
  after all napokon
  napokon, ipak *eepak*

afternoon popodne *popodne*

again opet *opet*

agency agencija *agentseeya*

agree (v) složiti se
  slozheetee se

ahead naprijed *napreeyed*,
  ispred *eespred*

aid pomoć *pomoch*
  first aid prva pomoć *prva
  pomoch*

air-conditioner klimatski uređaj *kleematskee oorejay*

airmail zračna pošta *zrachna poshta*

air mattress zračni madrac *zrachnee madrats*

airport zračna luka *zrachna looka*

alarm clock budilica *boodeeleetsa*

alcoholic drink alkoholno piće *alkoholno peeche*

all sav *sav*

not at all nikako *neekako*

allergy alergija *alergeeya*

allow (v) dopustiti *dopoosteetee*

almond badem *badem*

almost gotovo *gotovo*, umalo *oomalo*, skoro *skoro*

alone sam *sam*

also također *takojer*

always uvijek *ooveeyek*

am, (I) ja sam *ya sam*

ambulance kola hitne pomoći *kola heetne pomochee*

America Amerika *amereeka*

American američki *amereechkee*

American (m) Amerikanac *amereekanats*

American (f) Amerikanka *amereekanka*

amount iznos *eeznos*, svota *svota*

amuse (v) zabavljati (se) *zabavlyatee (se)*

anchor sidro *seedro*

and i *ee*, također *takojer*

angina pectoris angina pectoris *angeena pektorees*

angle udica *oodeetsa*

angry srdit *srdeet*, ljut *lyoot*

ankle gležanj *glezhany*

announcement najava *nayava*, objava *obyava*

annoy (v) ljutiti *lyooteetee*

that's annoying to čovjeka ljuti *to chovyeka lyootee*

answer (v) odgovoriti *odgovoreetee*

another drugi *droogee*, još jedan *yosh yedan*

anybody bilo tko *beelo tko*

anything bilo što *beelo shto*

apartment apartman *apartman*, stan *stan*

apologize (v) ispričati se *eespreechatee se*

appear (v) pojaviti se *poyaveetee se*

appendicitis upala slijepog crijeva *oopala sleeyepog creeyeva*

appetite apetit *apeteet*, tek *tek*

apple jabuka *yabooka*

application molba *molba*

appointement dogovor *dogovor*, termin *termeen*

apricot marelica *mareleetsa*

approve (v) odobriti *odobreetee*

April travanj *travany*, april *apreel*

are, (we) (mi) smo *(mee) smo*

are, (you) (vi) ste *(vee) ste*

are, (they) (oni/one/ona) su *(onee/one/ona) soo*

arm ruka *rooka*

armchair naslonjač *naslonyach*

around okolo *okolo*, naokolo *naokolo*

arrangement aranžman *aranzhman*; dogovor *dogovor*

make arrangements dogovoriti *dogovoreetee*

arrive (v) doći *dochee*, stići *steechee*

art umjetnost *oomyetnost*

as kao *kao*

ask (something) pitati (nešto) *peetatee (neshto)*

ask for zamoliti *zamoleetee*

at kod *kod*, u *oo*

at home kod kuće *kod kooche*

at 3 o'clock u tri sata *oo tree sata*

attention pažnja *pazhnya*

attractive privlačan *preevlachan*

August kolovoz *kolovoz*, august *aoogoost*

aunt tetka *tetka*

Australia Australija *aoostraleeya*

Australian australski *aoostralskee*

Australian (m) Australac *aoostralats*

Australian (f) Australka *aoostralka*

automobile automobil *aootomobeel*

autumn jesen *yesen*

available koji se može dobiti *koyee se mozhe dobeetee*

avoid (v) izbjegavati *eezbyegavatee*

away udaljen *oodalyen*; daleko *daleko*

it's 30 metres away to je udaljeno 30 metara *to ye oodalyeno treedeset metara*

it's far away to je daleko *to ye daleko*

awful grozan *grozan*

baby djetešce *dyeteshtse*

back (not in front) natrag *natrag*, otraga *otraga*; (body) leđa *leja*

backache bol u leđima *bol oo lejeema*

backpack ruksak *rooksak*, naprtnjača *naprtnyacha*

bacon slanina *slaneena*

bad zao *zao*, loš *losh*

bag torba *torba*
  handbag torbica *torbeetsa*

baggage prtljaga *prtlyaga*

bait mamac *mamats*

bake (v) peći *pechee*

baker pekar *pekar*

balcony balkon *balkon*

ball lopta *lopta*

ballet balet *balet*

banana banana *banana*

bandage zavoj *zavoj*; (strip) flaster *flaster*

bank banka *banka*

banknote novčanica *novchaneetsa*

barbecue roštilj *roshteely*

barber shop brijačnica *breeyachneetsa*

bargain jeftina kupnja *yefteena koopnya*

basket košara *koshara*

bathroom kupaonica *koopaoneetsa*

bathtub kada *kada*

bathe (v) kupati se *koopatee se*

battery baterija *batereeya*, akumulator *akoomoolator*

bay zaljev *zalyev*

be (v) biti *beetee*

beach plaža *plazha*

beans grah *grah*

beard brada *brada*

beautiful lijep *leeyep*, krasan *krasan*

beauty salon kozmetički salon *kozmeteechkee salon*

because jer *yer*, zato što *zato shto*

become (v) postati *postatee*

bed krevet *krevet*, postelja *postelya*

bedding posteljina *postelyeena*

bedroom spavaća soba *spavacha soba*

beef govedina *govedeena*

beer pivo *peevo*

before prije *preeye*

begin (v) početi *pochetee*

beginning početak *pochetak*

behind iza *eeza*, otraga *otraga*

believe (v) vjerovati *vyerovatee*

bell zvono *zvono*

belong (v) pripadati
preepadatee
below dolje *dolye*, ispod
eespod
belt pojas *poyas*
bench klupa *kloopa*
bend (road) zavoj *zavoy*,
okuka *okooka*
berth ležaj *lezhay*;
(naut) vez *vez*
beside pokraj *pokray*, do *do*
best najbolji *naybolyee*
better bolji *bolyee*
between između *eezmejoo*
beverage piće *peeche*,
napitak *napeetak*
bicycle bicikl *beetseekl*
big velik *veleek*
bill račun *rachoon*
bird ptica *pteetsa*
birthday rođendan
rojendan
biscuit keks *keks*
bit komadić *komadeech*;
malo *malo*
bite ugriz *oogreez*
bite (v) ugristi *oogreestee*
bitter gorak *gorak*
black crn *tsrn*
blanket pokrivač
pokreevach, deka *deka*
bleeding krvarenje *krvarenye*
blister mjehur *myehoor*,
plik, *pleek*

blocked blokiran *blokeeran*,
začepljen *zacheplyen*
blood krv *krv*
blood pressure krvni tlak
krvnee tlak
blouse bluza *blooza*
blow-dry (v) fenirati
feneeratee
blue plav *plav*, modar *modar*
blueberry borovnica
borovneetsa
board (v) ukrcati se
ookrtsatee se
boarding house pansion
panseeon
boat brod *brod*
boat trip putovanje brodom
pootovanye brodom
boat yard brodogradilište
brodogradeeleeshte; (small
port) lučica *loocheetsa*
body tijelo *teeyelo*
boil (v) kuhati *koohatee*
bone kost *kost*
book knjiga *knyeega*
booking rezervacija
rezervatseeya
booking office blagajna za
prodaju karata *blagayna za
prodayoo karata*
book shop knjižara
knyeezhara
boot čizma *cheezma*
border granica *graneetsa*

boss director *deerektor*, gazda *gazda*

both oba(dva) *oba (dva)*, oboje *oboye*

bother (v) dodijavati *dodeeyavatee*, gnjaviti *gnyaveetee*

bottle boca *botsa*, flaša *flasha*

bottle opener otvarač za boce *otvarach za botse*

bow (naut.) pramac *pramats*

bowl zdjela *zdyela*

box kutija *kooteeya*, sanduk *sandook*

boy dječak *dyechak*

boyfriend dečko *dechko*, momak *momak*

bracelet narukvica *narookveetsa*

brake kočnica *kochneetsa*

brake lights stop svjetla *stop svyetla*

branch (com) podružnica *podroozhneetsa*

bread kruh *krooh*

break (v) slomiti *slomeetee*

breakdown (car) kvar *kvar*

breakfast doručak *doroochak*

breathing difficulties smetnje u disanju *smetnye oo deesanyoo*

bridge most *most*

bright svijetao *sveeyetao*, sjajan *syayan*

bring (v) donijeti *doneeyetee*

British britanski *breetanskee*

brochure brošura *broshoora*

broken slomljen *slomlyen*

brooch broš *brosh*

brother brat *brat*

brown smeđ *smej*

brush četka *chetka*

building zgrada *zgrada*

bulb (light) žarulja *zharoolya*

bun pecivo *petseevo*

buoy plutača *plootacha*

burglar lopov *lopov*

burn opeklina *opekleena*

bus autobus *aootoboos*

bus station autobusni kolodvor *aootoboosnee kolodvor*

bus stop stajalište autobusa *stayaleeshte aootoboosa*

bus tour putovanje autobusom *pootovanye aootoboosom*

business posao *posao*, trgovanje *trgovanye*

business hours radno vrijeme *radno vreeyeme*

busy zaposlen *zaposlen*

but ali *alee*, nego *nego*

butcher mesar *mesar*

butter maslac *maslats*

buttock stražnjica *strazhnyeetsa*

button gumb *goomb*, puce *pootse*

buy (v) kupiti *koopeetee*

by do *do*, uz *ooz*
by tomorrow do sutra *do sootra*
by the window uz prozor *ooz prozor*
by day/night danju/noću *danyoo/nochoo*

cabbage zelje *zelye*, kupus *koopoos*
cabin kabina *kabeena*
café kavana *kavana*
cake kolač *kolach*, torta *torta*
calculate (v) računati *rachoonatee*
call (v) zvati *zvatee*; pozvati *pozvatee*
calm miran *meeran*
camera fotoaparat *fotoaparat*, kamera *kamera*
campground kamp *kamp*
can konzerva *konzerva*
can (v) moći *mochee*
can I mogu li *mogoo lee*
Canada Kanada *kanada*
Canadian kanadski *kanadskee*
Canadian (m) Kanađanin *kanajaneen*
Canadian (f) Kanađanka *kanajanka*

cancel (v) poništiti *poneeshteetee*
candle svijeća *sveeyecha*
candlestick svijećnjak *sveeyechnyak*
candy bombon *bombon*
cantaloupe dinja *deenya*
capable sposoban *sposoban*
car auto *aooto*
car ferry trajekt *trayekt*
car park parkiralište *parkeeraleeshte*
car wash autopraonica *aootopraoneetsa*
carburettor rasplinjač *raspleenyach*
card karta *karta*
care briga *breega*; pažnja *pazhnya*
care (v) brinuti se *breenootee se*, biti stalo *beetee stalo*
I don't care nije me briga *neeye me breega*
take care pazi na se *pazee na se*
careful pažljiv *pazhlyeev*
careless nemaran *nemaran*
carriage vagon *vagon*
carrot mrkva *mrkva*
carry (v) nositi *noseetee*
case kutija *kooteeya*; slučaj *sloochay*
cash gotovina *gotoveena*

cash machine bankomat *bankomat*

casino kasino *kaseeno*

casserole zdjela za kuhanje *zdyela za koohanye*; (meal) kuhano jelo u zdjeli *koohano yelo oo zdyelee*

cast anchor baciti sidro *batseetee seedro*

castle dvorac *dvorats*

cat mačka *machka*

catch (v) uhvatiti *oohvateetee*

cathedral katedrala *katedrala*

cauliflower karfiol *karfeeol*, cvjetača *tsvyetacha*

cause uzrok *oozrok*

caution oprez *oprez*

cave špilja *shpeelya*

cemetery groblje *groblye*

centre centar *tsentar*

cereals žitne pahuljice *zheetne pahoolyeetse*

certain siguran *seegooran*

certificate potvrda *potvrda*, svjedodžba *svyedojba*

chain lanac *lanats*

chair stolac *stolats*

chamber maid sobarica *sobareetsa*

chance prilika *preeleeka*

change (money) sitniš *seetneesh*

change (v) promijeniti *promeeyeneetee*

chapel kapela *kapela*

charge (v) zaračunati *zarachoonatee*

charming divan *deevan*, čaroban *charoban*

cheap jeftin *yefteen*

cheat (v) prevariti *prevareetee*

cheek obraz *obraz*, lice *leetse*

cheers živjeli *zheevyelee*

cheerful veseo *veseo*

cheese sir *seer*

chef glavni kuhar *glavnee koohar*

chemist ljekarnik *lyekarneek*, apotekar *apotekar*

cheque ček *chek*

cherry trešnja *treshnya*

cherry brandy šeri brendi *sheree brendee*

chest pain bol u prsima *bol oo prseema*

chewing gum žvakača guma *zhvakacha gooma*

chicken pile *peele*; (meat) piletina *peeleteena*

child dijete *deeyete*

children djeca *dyetsa*

chin (part of face) brada *brada*

china porculan *portsoolan*

chocolate čokolada *chokolada*

choose (v) izabrati *eezabratee*

church crkva *tsrkva*

cigarette cigareta *tseegareta*
cinema kino *keeno*
citizen stanovnik *stanovneek*
city grad *grad*
city centre središte grada
  sredeeshte grada
city map plan grada *plan
  grada*
class vrsta *vrsta*, razred *razred*
  first class prvorazredan
  prvorazredan
clean čist *cheest*
clear (bright) jasan *yasan*;
  (clean) bistar *beestar*
clear (v) (make empty)
  isprazniti *eesprazneetee*;
  (make tidy) pospremiti
  pospremeetee
clever pametan *pametan*
client klijent *kleeyent*
cliff greben *greben*
climate klima *kleema*
climb (v) penjati se
  penyatee se
clinic klinika *kleeneeka*
clock sat *sat*, ura *oora*
close (near) blizu *bleezoo*
close (v) zatvoriti *zatvoreetee*
clothes odjeća *odyecha*
cloudy oblačno *oblachno*
clutch spojka *spoyka*
coach autobus (za međugradski promet) *aootoboos
  (za mejoogradskee promet)*

coast obala *obala*
coat kaput *kapoot*
coffee kava *kava*
coin kovani novac *kovanee
  novats*
cold hladan *hladan*
cold cuts hladni naresci
  hladnee narestsee
collection kolekcija
  kolektseeya
collision sudar *soodar*
colour boja *boya*
colouring bojenje *boyenye*
coma koma *koma*
comb češalj *cheshaly*
come (v) doći *dochee*
  come back vratiti se
  vrateetee se
  come in ući *oochee*
  come from dolaziti iz
  dolazeetee eez
comfortable ugodan *oogodan*
commission provizija
  proveezeeya
company društvo *drooshtvo*
compare (v) usporediti
  oosporedeetee
compartment kupe *koope*,
  odjeljak *odyelyak*
compensation kompenzacija
  kompenzatseeya, odšteta
  odshteta
complain (v) potužiti se
  potoozheetee se

complete kompletan *kompletan*

complicated kompliciran *kompleetseeran*

computer kompjuter *kompyooter*, računalo *rachoonalo*

concert koncert *kontsert*

condition uvjet *oovyet*

conductor vozač *vozach*; (mus.) dirigent *deereegent*

congratulation čestitka *chesteetka*

confirm (v) potvrditi *potvrdeetee*

connect (v) spojiti *spoyeetee*

connection veza *veza*

consider (v) razmatrati *razmatratee*

consist (v) sastojati se *sastoyatee se*

consulate konzulat *konzoolat*

contact (v) kontaktirati *kontakteeratee*

contain (v) sadržavati *sadrzhavatee*

contact lenses kontaktne leće *kontaktne leche*

content zadovoljan *zadovolyan*

contract ugovor *oogovor*

contrary suprotan *sooprotan*
  on the contrary naprotiv *naproteev*

control kontrola *kontrola*

convenient pogodan *pogodan*

conversation razgovor *razgovor*

convulsion grčevi *grchevee*

cook (v) kuhati *koohatee*

cool hladan *hladan*; svjež *svyezh*

copper bakar *bakar*

corner ugao *oogao*, kut *koot*

correct ispravan *eespravan*

correction ispravak *eespravak*

correspondence dopisivanje *dopeeseevanye*

corridor hodnik *hodneek*

cost (v) koštati *koshtatee*

cost-free besplatan *besplatan*

cottage cheese kravlji sir *kravlyee seer*

cotton pamuk *pamook*

cotton wool vata *vata*

couch kauč *kaooch*

cough (v) kašljati *kashlyatee*

count (v) (find the total of) računati *rachoonatee*; (say numerals) brojiti *broyeetee*

counter pult *poolt*

country (state) država *drzhava*; (land) selo *selo*

couple dvoje *dvoye*, par *par*

courtyard dvorište *dvoreeshte*

cousin (m) bratić *brateech*

cousin (f) sestrična *sestreechna*

cover pokrivač *pokreevach*

cracker kreker *kreker*
cream vrhnje *vrhnye*
cream cheese sirni namaz
  seernee namaz
Croatia Hrvatska *hrvatska*
Croatian hrvatski *hrvatskee*
Croatian (m) Hrvat *hrvat*
Croatian (f) Hrvatica
  hrvateetsa
credit card kreditna kartica
  kredeetna karteetsa
crew posada *posada*
crossroads raskršće *raskrsh-che*, križanje *kreezhanye*
crowd gužva *goozhva*
cruise krstarenje *krstarenye*
cry (shout) vikati *veekatee*
crystal kristal *kreestal*
cucumber krastavac
  krastavats
cup šalica *shaleetsa*
curious radoznao *radoznao*
current tekući *tekoochee*
current account tekući
  račun *tekoochee rachoon*
curtain zavjesa *zavyesa*
customs carina *tsareena*
customs control carinska
  kontrola *tsareenska kontrola*
cut (v) rezati *rezatee*
cutlet kotlet *kotlet*
cutting rezanje *rezanye*
  hair cutting šišanje
  sheeshanye

daily dnevni *dnevnee*
Dalmatia Dalmacija
  dalmatseeya
Dalmatian dalmatinski
  dalmateenskee
Dalmatian (m) Dalmatinac
  dalmateenats
Dalmatian (f) Dalmatinka
  dalmateenka
damage šteta *shteta*
damp vlažan *vlazhan*
dance (v) plesati *plesatee*
dangerous opasan *opasan*
dare (v) usuditi se
  oosoodeetee se
dark taman *taman*
date datum *datoom*
daughter kćerka *kcherka*,
  kći *kchee*
day dan *dan*
  all day long cio dan
  tseeo dan
dead mrtav *mrtav*
dear drag *drag*
decaffeinated bez kofeina
  bez kofeeena
December prosinac
  proseenats, decembar
  detsembar
decent pristojan *preestoyan*,
  decentan *detsentan*
decide (v) odlučiti *odloocheetee*

decision odluka *odlooka*
deck paluba *palooba*
deckchair ležaljka *lezhalyka*
declare (v) deklarirati *deklareeratee*
decline (v) odbiti *odbeetee*
decoration dekoracija *dekoratseeya*
deep dubok *doobok*
definitive definitivan *defeeneeteevan*; konačan *konachan*
degree stupanj *stoopany*
delay (v) odgađati *odgajatee*
delicious izvrstan *eezvrstan*
delighted oduševljen *odooshevlyen*
  I'm delighted jako mi je drago *yako mee ye drago*
demand (v) zahtijevati *zahteeyevatee*
dentist zubar *zoobar*
deodorant dezodorans *dezodorans*
department store robna kuća *robna koocha*
departure odlazak *odlazak*
depend (v) ovisiti o *oveeseetee o*
  that depends to ovisi o *to oveesee o*
deposit (v) deponirati *deponeeratee*
describe (v) opisati *opeesatee*

deserve (v) zaslužiti *zasloozheetee*
dessert desert *desert*
determined odlučan *odloochan*
develop (v) razviti *razveetee*
diabetic coma dijabetička koma *deeyabeteechka koma*
diamond dijamant *deeyamant*
diarrhea proljev *prolyev*
dictionary rječnik *ryechneek*
die (v) umrijeti *oomreeyetee*
different različit *razleecheet*
difficult težak *tezhak*
digestion probava *probava*
dining room blagovaonica *blagovaoneetsa*
dinner večera *vechera*
direct (v) uputiti *oopooteetee*
direction smjer *smyer*
directory telefonski imenik *telefonskee eemeneek*
dirty prljav *prlyav*
disagree (v) ne slagati se *ne slagatee se*
disappear (v) nestati *nestatee*
disappointed razočaran *razocharan*
disco disko *deesko*
discount popust *popoost*
discover (v) otkriti *otkreetee*

discuss (v) diskutirati *deeskooteeratee*

discussion diskusija *deeskooseeya*

dish zdjela *zdyela*

distance udaljenost *oodalyenost*

disturb (v) uznemiriti *ooznemeereetee*

dive (v) roniti *roneetee*

divorced (m) rastavljen *rastavlyen*, (f) rastavljena *rastavlyena*

do (v) činiti *cheeneetee*; raditi *radeetee*

do a favour učiniti uslugu *oocheeneetee oosloogoo*

do the room spremati sobu *sprematee soboo*

dock dok *dok*

dock (v) biti u doku *beetee oo dokoo*

doctor doktor *doktor*, liječnik *leeyechneek*

doctor's office liječnička ordinacija *leeyechneechka ordeenatseeya*

document document *dokooment*

dog pas *pas*

doll lutka *lootka*

donkey magarac *magarats*

door vrata *vrata*

double dvostruko *dvostrooko*

doubtful sumnjičav *soomnyeechav*

doughnut uštipak *ooshteepak*

down dolje *dolye*

draw (v) vući *voochee*

dress haljina *halyeena*

drink (v) piti *peetee*

drink piće *peeche*

drive (v) voziti *vozeetee*

driver vozač *vozach*

driving licence vozačka dozvola *vozachka dozvola*

drop (v) ispustiti *eespoosteetee*

drug droga *droga*, lijek *leeyek*

drug overdose predoziranje *predozeeranye*

drugstore drogerija *drogereeya*

dry suh *sooh*

dry cleaning kemijsko čišćenje *kemeeysko cheeshchenye*

during za vrijeme *za vreeyeme*

dust prašina *prasheena*

duty dužnost *doozhnost*; carina *tsareena*

it's my duty to mi je dužnost *to mee ye doozhnost*

I've paid duty platio sam carinu *plateeo sam tsareenoo*

duty-free bez plaćanja carine *bez plachanya tsareene*

E

each svaki *svakee*
ear uho *ooho*
earache bol u uhu *bol oo oohoo*
early rano *rano*
earrings naušnice *naooshneetse*
earth Zemlja *zemlya*
east istok *eestok*
easy lagan *lagan*
eat (v) jesti *yestee*, pojesti *poyestee*
effort napor *napor*
egg jaje *yaye*
eggplant patlidžan *patleejan*
eight osam *osam*
eighteen osamnaest *osamnaest*
eighty osamdeset *osamdeset*
elbow lakat *lakat*
electric power električna struja *elektreechna strooya*
electricity elektricitet *elektreetseetet*
elevator lift *leeft*, dizalo *deezalo*
eleven jedanaest *yedanaest*
else inače *eenache*
  what else što još *shto yosh*
embark (v) ukrcati se *ookrtsatee se*

embarkation ukrcavanje *ookrtsavanye*
embassy ambasada *ambasada*, veleposlanstvo *veleposlanstvo*
embroidery vezenje *vezenye*
emergency opasnost *opasnost*
emergency aid hitna pomoć *heetna pomoch*
employ (v) zaposliti *zaposleetee*
empty prazan *prazan*
end kraj *kray*
engaged angažiran *angazheeran*, zauzet *zaoozet*
engaged (to be married) zaručen *zaroochen*
engine stroj *stroy*
England Engleska *engleska*
English engleski *engleskee*
Englishman Englez *englez*
Englishwoman Engleskinja *engleskeenya*
engine stroj *stroy*
enjoy (v) uživati u *oozheevatee oo*
enough dosta *dosta*
entertainment zabava *zabava*
entrance ulaz *oolaz*
envelope kuverta *kooverta*
environment okoliš *okoleesh*
equal jednak *yednak*

equipment oprema *oprema*
escalope odrezak *odrezak*
especially naročito
 narocheeto
essential bitan *beetan*
evening večer *vecher*
event dogadaj *dogajay*
ever ikada *eekada*
 forever zauvijek *zaooveeyek*
every svaki *svakee*
everybody svatko *svatko*
everything sve *sve*, svaka
 stvar *svaka stvar*
everywhere svuda *svooda*
example primjer *preemyer*
exactly točno *tochno*
except osim *oseem*
exchange (v) promijeniti
 promeeyeneetee
exchange office
 mjenjačnica *myenyachneetsa*
exchange rate devizni tečaj
 deveeznee techay
excellent izvrsno *eezvrsno*
excite (v) uzbuditi *oozboo-
 deetee*, uzrujati *oozrooyatee*
exciting experience
 uzbudljiv doživljaj
 oozboodlyeev dozheevlyay
excursion izlet *eezlet*
exhaust pipe ispušna cijev
 eespooshna ceeyev
excuse (v) ispričati (se)
 eespreechatee (se)

excuse me oprostite
 oprosteete
exist (v) egzistirati *egzees-
 teeratee*, postojati *postoyatee*
 it doesn't exist ne postoji
 ne postoyee
expect (v) očekivati
 ochekeevatee
expensive skup *skoop*
experience iskustvo
 eeskoostvo
expire (v) isteći *eestechee*
expiry date rok trajanja
 rok trayanya
explain (v) razjasniti
 razyasneetee
expression izraz *eezraz*
extend (v) produžiti
 prodoozheetee
extra dodatan *dodatan*
eye oko *oko*

face lice *leetse*
facial cream krema za lice
 krema za leetse
fact činjenica *cheenyeneetsa*
facilities oprema *oprema*,
 uređaji *oorejayee*
factory tvornica *tvorneetsa*
failure neuspjeh *neoospyeh*
fair fer *fer*, lijepo *leeyepo*
 fair play fer igra *fer*

eegra, poštena igra *poshtena eegra*

fair weather lijepo vrijeme *leeyepo vreeyeme*

fake falsifikat *falseefeekat*

fall (v) pasti *pastee*

fall (season) jesen *yesen*

family obitelj *obeetely*

familiar poznat *poznat*, naviknut na *naveeknoot na*

familiar face poznato lice *poznato leetse*

I'm familiar with upoznat sam sa *oopoznat sam sa*

famous slavan *slavan*

fan ventilator *venteelator*

fancy (v) svidjeti se *sveedyetee se*

fantastic fantastično *fantasteechno*

far dalek *dalek*

how far kako daleko *kako daleko*

farewell sretan put *sretan poot*

farm farma *farma*

fashion moda *moda*

fast brz *brz*

fat (food) mastan *mastan*

father otac *otats*

faucet pipa *peepa*

fault pogreška *pogreshka*

it's your fault vaša je pogreška *vasha ye pogreshka*

favour usluga *ooslooga*

favourable povoljan *povolyan*

fear strah *strah*

February veljača *velyacha*, februar *febrooar*

fee pristojba *preestoyba*

feel (v) osjećati *osyechatee*

I feel hot/cold meni je vruće/hladno *menee ye vrooche/hladno*

I don't feel well ne osjećam se dobro *ne osyecham se dobro*

fender (naut) bokobran *bokobran*

ferry prijevoz (trajektom) *preeyevoz(trayektom)*

ferry-boat trajekt *trayekt*

festivity svečanost *svechanost*

fever groznica *grozneetsa*

few nekoliko *nekoleeko*

fiancé zaručnik *zaroochneek*

fiancée zaručnica *zaroochneetsa*

field polje *polye*

fifteen petnaest *petnaest*

fifty pedeset *pedeset*

fig smokva *smokva*

fill (v) napuniti *napooneetee*

film film *feelm*

filter filter *feelter*

final konačan *konachan*

find (v) naći *nachee*

fine fin *feen*, krasan *krasan*

fine (traffic) globa *globa*

finger prst *prst*

fingernail nokat na ruci *nokat na rootsee*

finish (v) dovršiti *dovrsheetee*

finished gotov *gotov*

fire vatra *vatra*

fire-alarm protupožarni alarm *protoopozharnee alarm*

fire brigade vatrogasci *vatrogastsee*

firm čvrst *chvrst*

first prvi *prvee*

first aid prva pomoć *prva pomoch*

first class prvorazredan *prvorazredan*

fish riba *reeba*

  canned fish konzervirana riba *konzerveerana reeba*

fishing ribolov *reebolov*

fit sposoban *sposoban*; prikladan *preekladan*

  to keep fit održavati kondiciju *odrzhavatee kondeetseeyoo*

fitness fitnes *feetnes*, kondicija *kondeetseeya*

five pet *pet*

fix (v) popraviti *popraveetee*

flash fleš *flesh*

flat (apartment) stan *stan*

flat (level) ravno *ravno*

flavour okus *okoos*, aroma *aroma*

flight let *let*

flippers peraje *peraye*

floor kat *kat*

flour brašno *brashno*

flower cvijet *tsveeyet*

flower shop cvjećarnica *tsvyecharneetsa*

fly (v) letjeti *letyetee*

fog magla *magla*

folder prospekt *prospekt*

follow (v) ići za *eechee za*, slijediti *sleeyedeetee*

fond omiljen *omeelyen*

  I'm fond of him/her volim ga/je *voleem ga/ye*

food hrana *hrana*

foot noga *noga*

football nogomet *nogomet*

for za *za*, u *oo*

  for me za mene *za mene*

  for tonight za večeras *za vecheras*

  he's leaving for on odlazi u *on odlazee oo*

forest šuma *shooma*

foreigner stranac *stranats*

forget (v) zaboraviti
zaboraveetee

fork vilica *veeleetsa*

form formular *formoolar*;
oblik *obleek*

fortunately srećom *srechom*

fortune sreća *srecha*

four četiri *cheteeree*

fourteen četrnaest
chetrnaest

forty *chetrdeset*

fracture prijelom (kosti)
preeyelom (kostee)

free slobodan *slobodan*

French fries pomfrit
pomfreet

frequent čest *chest*

fresh svjež *svyezh*

fridge frižider *freezheeder*

fried pržen *przhen*

friend (m) prijatelj
preeyately

friend (f) prijateljica
preeyatelyeetsa

friendly prijateljski
preeyatelyskee

fritters fritule *freetoole*,
uštipci *ooshteepcee*

Friday petak *petak*

from od *od*, iz *eez*
  where are you from
  odakle ste *odakle ste*
  from Zagreb iz Zagreba
  eez zagreba

front prednja strana
prednya strana
  in front of sprijeda
  spreeyeda

fruit voće *voche*

fruit flavoured tea
voćni čaj *vochnee chay*

fruit juice voćni sok
vochnee sok

fry (v) peći *pechee*

fulfill (v) ispuniti
eespooneetee, udovoljiti
oodovolyeetee

full potpuno *potpoono*,
sasvim *sasveem*

fun zabava *zabava*,
užitak *oozheetak*
  for fun za šalu *za shaloo*

function (v) funkcionirati
foonktseeoneeratee; raditi
radeetee

function funkcija *foonk-
tseeya*; služba *sloozhba*

funny smiješan *smeeyeshan*

furious bijesan *beeyesan*

furnished room namještena
soba *namyeshtena soba*

furniture pokućstvo
pokoochstvo

future budućnost
boodoochnost
  in the future ubuduće
  ooboodooche

G

gale oluja *olooya*

gallery galerija *galereeya*

gambling kockanje *kotskanye*

game igra *eegra*

gangway ulaz na brod *oolaz na brod*

garage garaža *garazha*

garden vrt *vrt*

garlic češnjak *cheshnyak*

gas (for heating) plin *pleen*; (petrol) benzin *benzeen*

gate (entrance) prilaz *preelaz*, (door) vrata *vrata*

gather (v) skupiti *skoopeetee*

gears brzine *brzeene*

general (not special) opće-nit *opcheneet*, (common) uobičajen *ooobeechayen*

generally općenito *opcheneeto*

gentle blag *blag*, nježan *nyezhan*

gentleman gospodin *gospodeen*

genuine autentičan *aootenteechan*, nepatvoren *nepatvoren*

get (v) (obtain) dobiti *do-beetee*; (have) imati *eematee*

get back vratiti se *vrateetee se*

get down sići *seechee*

get in ući *oochee*

get out izaći *eezachee*

get together sastati se *sastatee se*

get up ustati *oostatee*

gift dar *dar*

gift shop prodavaonica darova *prodavaoneetsa darova*

gin džin *jeen*

girl djevojka *dyevoyka*

girlfriend djevojka *dyevoyka*, cura *tsoora*

give (v) dati *datee*

give back vratiti *vrateetee*

give up odreći se *odrechee se*

glad radostan *radostan*

I'm glad drago mi je *drago mee ye*

glass staklo *staklo*; (for drinking) čaša *chasha*

glasses naočale *naochale*

go (v) ići *eechee*, poći *pochee*

go away otići *oteechee*

go in ući *oochee*

go on ići dalje *eechee dalye*

go out izići *eezeechee*

God Bog *bog*

gold zlato *zlato*

good dobar *dobar*

goodbye zbogom *zbogom*

government vlada *vlada*, državna uprava *drzhavna ooprava*

granddaughter unuka
oonooka

grandfather djed *dyed*

grandmother baka *baka*

grandson unuk *oonook*

gratis gratis *gratees*,
besplatno *besplatno*

gratitude zahvalnost
zahvalnost

gratuity napojnica
napoyneetsa

gravy umak (od pečenke)
oomak (od pechenke)

greasy mastan *mastan*

great velik *veleek*

Great Britain Velika Britanija *veleeka breetaneeya*

green zelen *zelen*

greeting pozdrav *pozdrav*

grey siv *seev*

grill roštilj *roshteely*

grilled pečen na roštilju
pechen na roshteelyoo

grocery store prodavaonica
mješovite robe *prodavaoneetsa myeshoveete robe*

groundfloor prizemlje
preezemlye

group grupa *groopa*

guarantee garancija
garantseeya

guest gost *gost*

guesthouse pansion
panseeon

guide vodič *vodeech*

guide book vodič (knjiga)
vodeech

guided tour obilazak s vo-
dičem *obeelazak s vodeechem*

gulf zaljev *zalyev*

gym gimnastička dvorana
geemnasteechka dvorana

habit navika *naveeka*

hair kosa *kosa*

hairdresser frizer *freezer*

hair dryer fen *fen*

half pola *pola*

half a kilo pola kile *pola
keele*

half price u pola cijene
oo pola tseeyene

hall dvorana *dvorana*

halt (v) zaustaviti se
zaoostaveetee se

ham šunka *shoonka*

hamburger hamburger
hamboorger

hand ruka *rooka*

at hand pri ruci *pree
rootsee*

handicraft rukotvorina
rookotvoreena

handle ručka *roochka*

handmade ručni rad
roochnee rad

handsome lijep *leeyep*, zgodan *zgodan*

hanger vješalica *vyeshaleetsa*

happen (v) dogoditi se *dogodeetee se*

  what happened što se dogodilo *shto se dogodeelo*

happening događaj *dogajay*

happy sretan *sretan*

harbour luka *looka*

hard (firm) tvrd *tvrd*; (difficult) težak *tezhak*

hat šešir *shesheer*

haul (v) vući *voochee*, tegliti *tegleetee*

have (v) imati *eematee*

  have back dobiti natrag *dobeetee natrag*

have a good time dobro se provesti *dobro se provestee*

hazelnut lješnjak *lyeshnyak*

he on *on*

head glava *glava*

headache glavobolja *glavobolya*

headlight veliko svjetlo *veleeko svyetlo*

healthy zdravo *zdravo*

hear (v) čuti *chootee*

heart srce *srtse*

heart attack srčani udar *srchanee oodar*

heat vrućina *vroocheena*

heating grijanje *greeyanye*

heavy težak *tezhak*

heel peta *peta*

herb brandy travarica *travareetsa*

help (v) pomoći *pomochee*

her nju *nyoo*, njoj *nyoy*; njezin *nyezeen*

  for her za nju *za nyoo*

  to her njoj *nyoy*

  her room njezina soba *nyezeena soba*

here ovdje *ovdye*

high visok *veesok*

highlights (hair colouring) pramenovi *pramenovee*

hiking pješačenje *pyeshachenye*

highway autocesta *aoototsesta*

hill brežuljak *brezhoolyak*

him njega *nyega*, njemu *nyemoo*

  for him za njega *za nyega*

  to him njemu *nyemoo*

hire (v) iznajmiti *eeznaymeetee*, unajmiti *oonaymeetee*

his njegov *nyegov*

historical povijesni *poveeyesnee*

hit (v) udariti *oodareetee*

hold (v) držati *drzhatee*

hole rupa *roopa*

holiday blagdan *blagdan*

holidays praznici *prazneetsee*, dopust *dopoost*

home dom *dom*, kuća
koocha

honest pošten *poshten*

honey med *med*

honeymoon medeni mjesec
medenee myesets

honour čast *chast*,
poštovanje *poshtovanye*

hook kuka *kooka*

hope nada *nada*

horn rog *rog*

horrible užasan *oozhasan*

horse konj *kony*

hospital bolnica *bolneetsa*

hospitality gostoljubivost
gostolyoobeevost

hot vruć *vrooch*

hotel hotel *hotel*

hour sat *sat*

house kuća *koocha*

how kako *kako*

  how much koliko *koleeko*

hungry gladan *gladan*

hurry (v) žuriti se *zhooreetee
se*, požuriti se *pozhooreetee se*

  in a hurry u žurbi *oo
zhoorbee*

hurt (v) (injure) ozlijediti
ozleeyedeetee; (pain) boljeti
bolyetee

husband suprug *sooproog*,
muž *moozh*

hydrofoil hidrogliser
heedrogleeser

I ja *ya*

ice led *led*

ice cream sladoled *sladoled*

ice cube kockica leda
kotskeetsa leda

ice tea ledeni čaj *ledenee chay*

identity identitet *eedenteetet*

if ako *ako*; da *da*

  if you come ako dođeš
ako dojesh

  if I were you da sam na
tvom mjestu *da sam na
tvom myestoo*

ill bolestan *bolestan*

immediately odmah
odmah, smjesta *smyesta*

import uvoz *oovoz*

importance važnost *vazhnost*

important važan *vazhan*

impossible nemoguć
nemogooch

improve (v) poboljšati
pobolyshatee

in u *oo*, na *na*, za *za*

  in the room u sobi *oo
sobee*

  in Croatian na hrvatskom
na hrvatskom

  in an hour za jedan sat *za
yedan sat*

inadequate nedovoljan
nedovolyan

incident izgred *eezgred*, nemio slučaj *nemeeo sloochay*

inclusive uračunato *oorachoonato*

all inclusive sve uključeno (u cijenu) *sve ooklyoocheno (oo tseeyenoo)*

incomplete nepotpun *nepotpoon*

incorrect netočan *netochan*

increase (v) povećati (se) *povechatee (se)*

incredible nevjerojatan *nevyeroyatan*

indefinite neograničen *neograneechen*

independent samostalan *samostalan*

indicate (v.) pokazivati *pokazeevatee*

individual individualan *eendeeveedooalan*, zaseban *zaseban*

inexpensive jeftin *yefteen*

inexperienced neiskusan *neeeskoosan*, bez prakse *bez prakse*

infection infekcija *eenfektseeya*, zaraza *zaraza*

influence utjecaj *ootyetsay*

inform (v) informirati *eenformeeratee*, obavijestiti *obaveeyesteetee*

information informacija *eenformatseeya*, obavijest *obaveeyest*

inhabitant stanovnik *stanovneek*

injection injekcija *eenyektseeya*

injury ozljeda *ozlyeda*

injured ozlijeđen *ozleeyejen*

inn gostionica *gosteeoneetsa*

innocent nedužan *nedoozhan*

inquire (v) raspitati se *raspeetatee se*

insect insekt *eensekt*, kukac *kookats*

insect repellent sprej protiv insekata *sprey proteev eensekata*

inside unutra *oonootra*

insist (v) inzistirati *eenzeesteeratee*

instead umjesto *oomyesto*

instruct (v) uputiti *oopooteetee*

insufficient nedostatan *nedostatan*

insult (v) uvrijediti *oovreeyedeetee*

insurance osiguranje *oseegooranye*

interest interes *eenteres*, zanimanje za *zaneemanye za*

interesting zanimljivo *zaneemlyeevo*

interfere (v) upletati se *oopletatte se*

internal unutrašnji *oonootrashnyee*

international međunarodni *mejoonarodnee*

international call međunarodni poziv *mejoonarodnee pozeev*

interpret (v) tumačiti *toomacheetee*, usmeno prevoditi *oosmeno prevodeetee*

interrupt (v) prekidati *prekeedatee*

introduce (v) predstaviti *predstaveetee*

instead umjesto *oomyesto*

invalid invalid *eenvaleed*

inventory inventar *eenventar*

invite (v) pozvati *pozvatee*

Ireland Irska *eerska*

Irish (m) Irac *eerats*

Irish (f) Irkinja *eerkeenya*

Irish irski *eerskee*

iron pegla *pegla*, glačalo *glachalo*

is, (he/she/it) je (on/ona/ono) *ye (on/ona/ono)*

island otok *otok*

it ono *ono*

itinerary itinerer *eeteenerer*; ruta *roota*

jacket jakna *yakna*

jam džem *jem*

January siječanj *seeyechany*, januar *yanooar*

jeans traperice *trapereetse*

jelly žele *zhele*

jellyfish meduza *medooza*

jeweller zlatar *zlatar*

jewellery nakit *nakeet*

job posao *posao*

join (v) priključiti se *preeklyoocheetee se*, pridruži-ti se *preedroozheetee se*

may I join you mogu li se pridružiti *mogoo lee se preedroozheetee*

joke šala *shala*

journey put *poot*, putovanje *pootovanye*

joy veselje *veselye*

joyful veseo *veseo*

judge sudac *soodats*

juice sok *sok*

July srpanj *srpany*, juli *yoolee*

jump (v) skakati *skakatee*, skočiti *skocheetee*

June lipanj *leepany*, juni *yoonee*

just upravo *oopravo*, baš *bash*

just now baš sada *bash sada*

K

keep (v) čuvati *choovatee*, održavati *odrzhavatee*
  keep off ne dati blizu *ne datee bleezoo*
  keep up podržavati *podrzhavatee*
key ključ *klyooch*
kind ljubazan *lyoobazan*
  be so kind budite ljubazni *boodeete lyoobaznee*
  it's very kind of you vrlo ste ljubazni *vrlo ste lyoobaznee*
kiss (v) poljubiti *polyoobeetee*
kitchen kuhinja *kooheenya*
kitchenette kuhinjica *kooheenyeetsa*
knife nož *nozh*
knee koljeno *kolyeno*
knitting pletivo *pleteevo*
knock (v) kucati *kootsatee*
knot čvor *chvor*
know (v) znati *znatee*, poznati *poznatee*
  I know where it is znam gdje je to *znam gdye ye to*
  she knows me ona me poznaje *ona me poznaye*

L

label etiketa *eteeketa*
lace čipka *cheepka*
ladle kutlača *kootlacha*
lady dama *dama*, gospođa *gospoja*
lake jezero *yezero*
lamb (meat) janjetina *yanyeteena*; (animal) janje *yanye*
lamp svjetiljka *svyeteelyka*
land kopno *kopno*, zemlja *zemlya*
landing (ship) iskrcavanje *eeskrtsavanye*; (aircraft) prizemljenje *preezemlyenye*
landlady gazdarica *gazdareetsa*, stanodavka *stanodavka*
landlord gazda *gazda*, stanodavac *stanodavats*
landscape pejsaž *peysazh*; krajolik *krayoleek*
language jezik *yezeek*
large velik *veleek*
last (v) trajati *trayatee*
last posljednji *poslyednyee*, zadnji *zadnyee*, prošli *proshlee*
  last call posljednji poziv *poslyednyee pozeev*
  last week prošli tjedan *proshlee tyedan*

late kasan *kasan*, prekasan
prekasan

  it's late kasno je *kasno ye*

  he's late on je zakasnio *on
ye zakasneeo*

later kasnije *kasneeye*

laugh smijati se *smeeyatee se*

laundry (dirty clothes) prljavo rublje *prlyavo rooblye*

laurel lovor *lovor*

lavatory toalet *toalet*,
zahod *zahod*

lavender lavanda *lavanda*

lawyer odvjetnik *odvyetneek*,
advokat *advokat*

lawn travnjak *travnyak*

lead (v) voditi *vodeetee*

lean meat nemasno meso
nemasno meso

learn (v) učiti *oocheetee*

lease (v) zakupiti *zakoopeetee*, unajamiti *oonaymeetee*

least najmanje *naymanye*

  not in the least
ni najmanje *nee naymanye*

leather (goods) (predmeti)
od kože *(predmetee) od kozhe*

leave (v) otići *oteechee*,
napustiti *napoosteetee*

leek poriluk *poreelook*

left lijevo *leeyevo*

  turn left skreni lijevo
skrenee leeyevo

leg noga *noga*

lemon limun *leemoon*

lend (v) posuditi *posoodeetee*

less manji *manyee*

lesson poduka *podooka*,
lekcija *lektseeya*

let (v) dopustiti *dopoosteetee*

  let me go pusti me
poostee me

letter pismo *peesmo*

lettuce zelena salata *zelena
salata*

licence dozvola *dozvola*

lie (v) ležati *lezhatee*

  lie down leći *lechee*

life život *zheevot*

life boat čamac za spašavanje
chamats za spashavanye

life jacket pojas za spašavanje *poyas za spashavanye*

lift lift *leeft*, dizalo *deezalo*

light svjetlo *svyetlo*

lighthouse svjetionik
svyeteeoneek

like (v) voljeti *volyetee*

  how do you like it kako ti se
to sviđa *kako tee se to sveeja*

line linija *leeneeya*, crta *tsrta*

line (rope) konop *konop*

linen lanen *lanen*; posteljina
postelyeena

lip usna *oosna*

liquid tekućina *tekoocheena*

listen (v) slušati *slooshatee*

litre litra *leetra*

little malen *malen*

live (v) živjeti *zheevyetee*

lively živahan *zheevahan*

living room dnevna soba *dnevna soba*

lobby predvorje (u hotelu) *predvorye*

local mjesni *myesnee*

locals mještani *myeshtanee*

location lokacija *lokatseeya*

lock brava *brava*

lodgings iznajmljeni stan *eeznaymlyenee stan*

long dug *doog*

all day long cio dan *tseeo dan*

look (v) pogledati *pogledatee*, gledati *gledatee*

look after pripaziti na *preepazeetee na*

look at promatrati *promatratee*

look for tražiti (nešto) *trazheetee (neshto)*

loose labav *labav*

lose (v) izgubiti *eezgoobeetee*

loss of consciousness gubitak svijesti *goobeetak sveeyestee*

lost izgubljen *eezgooblyen*

loud glasan *glasan*

lounge društvena prostorija (u hotelu) *drooshtvena prostoreeya*

lounge chair naslonjač *naslonyach*

love (v) voljeti *volyetee*, biti zaljubljen *beetee zalyooblyen*

love ljubav *lyoobav*

fall in love zaljubiti se *zalyoobeeteese*

low nizak *neezak*

luck sreća *srecha*

luggage prtljaga *prtlyaga*

lunch ručak *roochak*

luxurious luksuzan *looksoozan*

made izrađen *eezrajen*, načinjen *nacheenyen*

magazine časopis *chasopees*

mail pošta *poshta*; (v) poslati (poštom) *poslatee (poshtom)*

maid sobarica *sobareetsa*

main glavni *glavnee*

maintain (v) održavati *odrzhavatee*

make (v) činiti *cheeneetee*, izraditi *eezradeetee*

make an appointment ugovoriti sastanak *oogovoreetee sastanak*

make a mistake pogriješiti *pogreeyesheetee*

make money zarađivati *zarajeevatee*

make a phone call
telefonirati *telefoneerate*
make-up šminka *shmeenka*
man čovjek *chovyek*
manager direktor *deerektor*,
upravitelj *oopraveetely*
management uprava *ooprava*
many mnogi *mnogee*
map karta *karta*, plan *plan*
marble mramor *mramor*
March ožujak *ozhooyak*,
mart *mart*
margarine margarin
margareen
marina marina *mareena*
mark označiti *oznacheetee*
market tržnica *trzhneetsa*
farmers' market tržnica
na otvorenom *trzhneetsa
na otvorenom*
married (m) oženjen
ozhenyen
married (f) udana *oodana*
mass misa *meesa*
mast jarbol *yarbol*
match (v) slagati se, *slagatee
se*, usporediti *oosporedeetee*
the colours don't match
boje se ne slažu *boye se ne
slazhoo*
she can't match him
ona se ne može s njim
usporediti *ona se ne mozhe
s nyeem oosporedeetee*

matter svar *stvar*
what's the matter što je
shto ye
May svibanj *sveebany*, maj
may
may (v) moći *mochee*
may I ask you something?
mogu li vas nešto pitati?
*mogoo lee vas neshto
peetatee*
maybe možda *mozhda*
me mene *mene*, meni *menee*
the letter is for me
pismo je za mene *peesmo
ye za mene*
give it to me daj ga meni
day ga menee
meal obrok *obrok*
mean (v) značiti *znacheetee*
meaning značenje *znachenye*
measure mjera *myera*
meat meso *meso*
mechanic mehaničar
mehaneechar
medication lijek *leeyek*
medium srednji *srednyee*
meet (v) sresti (se) *srestee
(se)*, upoznati *oopoznatee*
I met her in the street
srela sam je na ulici *srela
sam ye na ooleetsee*
we've already met mi
smo se već upoznali *mee
smo se vech oopoznalee*

meeting sastanak *sastanak*

melon dinja *deenya*

member član *chlan*

menu jelovnik *yelovneek*

mess nered *nered*

message poruka *porooka*

middle sredina *sredeena*

midnight ponoć *ponoch*

migraine migrena
meegrena

milk mlijeko *mleeyeko*

mind (v) biti stalo do *beetee stalo do*, obazirati se
obazeeratee se

  I don't mind nije mi stalo
  neeye mee stalo

  never mind ništa zato
  neeshta zato

mine moj *moy*, moja *moya*,
moje *moye*

mineral water mineralna
voda *meeneralna voda*

minute minuta *meenoota*

miracle čudo *choodo*

mirror ogledalo *ogledalo*,
zrcalo, *zrtsalo*

miserable jadan *yadan*

misfortune nesreća
nesrecha

miss (v) nedostajati
nedostayatee; propustiti
propoosteetee

  I miss you nedostaješ mi
  nedostayesh mee

**he missed the opportu-
nity** propustio je priliku
propoosteeo ye preeleekoo

missing nestao *nestao*

mistake pogreška *pogreshka*

  by mistake zabunom
  zaboonom

mister gospodin *gospodeen*

misunderstand (v) krivo
razumjeti *kreevo
razoomjetee*

mix (v) (po)miješati
(po)meeyeshatee

mobile home kamp-prikolica
kamp-preekoleetsa

mobile phone mobitel
mobeetel

moderate umjeren *oomyeren*

moment moment *moment*,
trenutak *trenootak*

monastery samostan
samostan

Monday ponedjeljak
ponedyelyak

money novac *novats*

month mjesec *myesets*

monument spomenik
spomeneek

moon mjesec *myesets*

moor (v) usidriti brod
ooseedreetee brod

more više *veeshe*

  a little more malo više
  malo veeshe

mosquito komarac *komarats*

morning jutro *yootro*

most najviše *nayveeshe*

  most of all najviše od svega *nayveeshe od svega*

mother majka *mayka*

motorcycle motocikl *mototseekl*

motorboat motorni čamac *motornee chamats*

mountain planina *planeena*

mouth usta *oosta*

move (v) krenuti *krenootee*, maknuti se *maknootee se*

  move in useliti se *ooseleetee se*

  move out iseliti se *eeseleetee se*

movie film *feelm*

movie theater kino *keeno*

much mnogo *mnogo*

  not so much ne toliko *ne toleeko*

  too much previše *preveeshe*

mug krigla *kreegla*, vrč *vrch*

mule mazga *mazga*

museum muzej *moozey*

mushroom gljiva *glyeeva*

music glazba *glazba*

must morati *moratee*

mustard senf *senf*

my (m) moj *moy*, (f) moja *moya*, (n) moje *moye*

nail nokat *nokat*

nail polish lak za nokte *lak za nokte*

naked gol *gol*

name ime *eeme*, naziv *nazeev*

  first (given) name ime *eeme*

  family name prezime *prezeeme*

napkin salveta *salveta*, ubrus *oobroos*

narrow uzak *oozak*

national park nacionalni park *natseeonalnee park*

natives domaće stanovništvo *domache stanovneeshtvo*

natural prirodan *preerodan*

navigation navigacija *naveegatseeya*

near blizu *bleezoo*

nearby obližnji *obleezhnyee*

neat uredan *ooredan*, čist *cheest*

necessary nužan *noozhan*, potreban *potreban*

necklace ogrlica *ogrleetsa*

nectarine nektarina *nektareena*

need (v) trebati *trebatee*

needle igla *eegla*

negative negativ *negateev*

negotiate pregovarati *pregovaratee*

neighbour (m) susjed *soosyed*

neighbour (f) susjeda *soosyeda*

neither ni jedan *nee yedan*

neither of us ni jedan od nas *nee yedan od nas*

never nikada *neekada*

new nov *nov*

news novosti *novostee*

news stand novinski kiosk *novinski keeosk*

New Zealand Novi Zeland *novee zeland*

New Zealander (m) Novozelanđanin *novozelanjaneen*

New Zealander (f) Novozelanđanka *novozelanjanka*

New Zealand (of) novozelandski *novozelandskee*

next sljedeći *slyedechee*, pored *pored*

next week sljedeći tjedan *slyedechee tyedan*

sit next to me sjedi pored mene *syedee pored mene*

nice prijazan *preeyazan*, ugodan *oogodan*

night noć *noch*

night club noćni local *nochnee lokal*, bar *bar*

nine devet *devet*

nineteen devetnaest *devetnaest*

ninety devedeset *devedeset*

no (not) ne *ne*

no, thank you ne, hvala *ne hvala*

no way nikako *neekako*

noisy bučan *boochan*

noon podne *podne*

non-alcoholic drink bezalkoholno piće *bezalkoholno peeche*

none ni jedan *nee yedan*

normally obično *obeechno*

note (v) pribilježiti *preebeelyezheetee*

notebook bilježnica *beelyezhneetsa*

nothing ništa *neeshta*

notice (v) opaziti *opazeetee*, primijetiti *preemeeyeteetee*

nose nos *nos*

November studeni *stoodenee*, novembar *novembar*

now sada *sada*

nowhere nigdje *neegdye*

nudist nudist *noodeest*

nuisance neugodnost *neoogodnost*

what a nuisance kakva neprilika *kakva nepreeleeka*

number broj *broy*

numerous mnogobrojan *mnogobroyan*

nurse medicinska sestra *medeetseenska sestra*

o

oar veslo *veslo*
object (v) prigovoriti *preegovoreetee*
object predmet *predmet*
obligation obaveza *obaveza*
observe (v) promatrati *promatratee*
obstacle smetnja *smetnya*
obtain (v) dobiti *dobeetee*
obvious očit *ocheet*, jasan *yasan*
occasion prilika *preeleeka*, zgoda *zgoda*
occasionally povremeno *povremeno*
occupation zvanje *zvanye*
occupy (v) zauzeti *zaoozetee*
odd čudan *choodan*
odour miris *meerees*, smrad *smrad*
of od *od*
offence prekršaj *prekrshay*; uvreda *oovreda*
  (legal) offence prekršaj (zakona) *prekrshay (zakona)*
  it was an offence to je bila uvreda *to ye beela oovreda*
offer (v) ponuditi (se) *ponoodeetee (se)*

office ured *oored*
officer službenik *sloozhbeneek*, policajac *poleetsayats*
official služben *sloozhben*
often često *chesto*
oil ulje *oolye*
olive oil maslinovo ulje *masleenovo oolye*
olive maslina *masleena*
old star *star*
omit (v) propustiti *propoosteetee*
on na *na*, u *oo*
  on the table na stolu *na stoloo*
  on Friday u petak *oo petak*
once jednom *yednom*
one jedan *yedan*
one-way ticket putna karta u jednom smjeru *pootna karta oo yednom smyeroo*
onion luk *look*
only samo *samo*
open (v) otvoriti *otvoreetee*
open otvoreno *otvoreno*
opening otvorenje *otvorenye*
opera opera *opera*
operator telefonist *telefoneest*
opinion mišljenje *meeshlyenye*
opportunity (povoljna) prilika *(povolyna) preeleeka*

opposite suprotan *sooprotan*

optional fakultativan *fakooltateevan*, izboran *izboran*

or ili *eelee*

orange naranča *narancha*

order (v) naručiti *naroocheetee*, zapovjediti *zapovyedeetee*

  he ordered a taxi naručio je taksi *naroocheeo ye taksee*

  she ordered him to go zapovjedila mu je da ode *zapovyedeela moo ye da ode*

order narudžba *naroojba*

organize (v) organizirati *organeezeeratee*

original izvorni *eezvornee*, originalan *oreegeenalan*

other drugi *droogee*, drukčiji *drookcheeyee*

otherwise na drugi način *na droogee nacheen*

our (m) naš *nash*, (f) naša *nasha*, (n) naše *nashe*

out van *van*, vani *vanee*

outdated zastario *zastareeo*

outside vanjski *vanyskee*

oven pećnica *pechneetsa*

over preko *preko*, (iz)nad *(eez)nad*

overboard u more (iz broda) *oo more (eez broda)*

overcharge (v) previše zaračunati *preveeshe zarachoonatee*

overdue zakasnio *zakasneeo*

own (v) posjedovati *posyedovatee*, imati *eematee*

owner vlasnik *vlasneek*

package paket *paket*, zamotak *zamotak*

packing pakiranje *pakeeranye*

page stranica *straneetsa*

painful bolan *bolan*

pain bol *bol*

paint (v) slikati *sleekatee*

painting slika *sleeka*

pair par *par*

palace palača *palacha*

pale blijed *bleeyed*

pancake palačinka *palacheenka*

pants hlače *hlache*

paper papir *papeer*

papers novine *noveene*; (documents) isprave *eesprave*

parasol suncobran *soontsobran*

parcel paket *paket*

pardon (me) molim *moleem*

parents roditelji *rodeetelyee*

park (v) parkirati *parkeeratee*

park (public garden) park *park*; (car) parkiralište *parkeeraleeshte*

part dio *deeo*

  take a part in sudjelovati u *soodyelovatee oo*

participant sudionik *soodeeoneek*

party zabava *zabava*

parsley peršin *persheen*

pass (v) proći *prochee*, provesti *provestee*

  pass by prolaziti *prolazeetee*

pass propusnica *propoosneetsa*

passage prolaz *prolaz*; (voyage) plovidba *ploveedba*

passenger putnik *pootneek*

past prošao *proshao*

  in times past u prošlosti *oo proshlostee*

pasta tjestenina *tyesteneena*, pašta *pashta*

pastry shop slastičarnica *slasteecharneetsa*

path staza *staza*, put *poot*

patient pacijent *patseeyent*, bolesnik *bolesneek*

pattern uzorak *oozorak*

pavement pločnik *plochneek*

pay (v) platiti *plateetee*

  pay in uplatiti *ooplateetee*

  pay out isplatiti *eesplateetee*

peace mir *meer*

peach breskva *breskva*

pear kruška *krooshka*

peas grašak *grashak*

peasant seljak *selyak*

pebble oblutak *oblootak*

peculiar čudan *choodan*, neobičan *neobeechan*

pedestrian pješak *pyeshak*

people ljudi *lyoodee*, narod *narod*

pepper (for seasoning) papar *papar*; (plant) paprika *papreeka*

per po *po*

  per day po danu *po danu*

  per post poštom *poshtom*

perfect perfektan *perfektan*, savršen *savrshen*

performance predstava *predstava*

perfume parfem *parfem*

perhaps možda *mozhda*

permanent stalan *stalan*

permission dozvola *dozvola*

permit (v) dopustiti *dopoosteetee*

persist (v) ustrajati *oostrayatee*, ne popustiti *ne popoosteetee*

person osoba *osoba*

personal osobni *osobnee*

personnel osoblje *osoblye*

persuade (v) nagovoriti *nagovoreetee*

pet ljubimac *lyoobeemats*

petrol benzin *benzeen*

pharmacist ljekarnik *lyekarneek*, apotekar *apotekar*

pharmacy ljekarna *lyekarna*, apoteka *apoteka*

photo fotografija *fotografeeya*

photographer fotograf *fotograf*

phrase fraza *fraza*, izraz *eezraz*

pick up (v) pokupiti (putnike) *pokoopeetee (pootneeke)*

picture slika *sleeka*

piece komad *komad*

pier molo *molo*

pill pilula *peeloola*

pillow jastuk *yastook*

pity samilost *sameelost*

it's a pity šteta *shteta*

place (v) staviti *staveetee*

place mjesto *myesto*

in place of umjesto *oomyesto*

plain jednostavan *yednostavan*

plan plan *plan*

plant biljka *beelyka*

plate tanjur *tanyoor*

play (v) igrati *eegratee*, svirati *sveeratee*

play tennis igrati tenis *eegratee tenees*

play the piano svirati glasovir *sveeratee glasoveer*

play igra *eegra*, kazališni komad *kazaleeshnee komad*

playground igralište *eegraleeshte*

pleasant ugodan *oogodan*, prijatan *preeyatan*

please (v) biti drago *beetee drago*, ugoditi *oogodeetee*

I'm pleased with it meni je to drago *menee ye to drago*

he's hard to please teško mu je ugoditi *teshko moo ye oogodeetee*

show it to me, please pokažite mi to, molim vas *pokazheete mee to moleem vas*

pleasure zadovoljstvo *zadovolystvo*

plenty puno *poono*

plug utikač *ooteekach*

plum šljiva *shlyeeva*

plum brandy šljivovica *shlyeevoveetsa*

pocket džep *jep*

poisoning trovanje *trovanye*

police policija *poleetseeya*

polite uljudan *oolyoodan*

pool bazen *bazen*

poor siromašan *seeromashan*

popular popularan
popoolaran

pork svinjetina *sveenyeteena*

port luka *looka*

  make port stići u luku
  steechee oo lookoo

  clear port isploviti iz luke
  eesploveetee eez looke

port side (naut.) lijevi bok
leeyevee bok

porter nosač *nosach*; vratar
vratar

position položaj *polozhay*

positive pozitivan
pozeeteevan

possess (v) posjedovati
posyedovatee, imati *eematee*

possibility mogućnost
mogoochnost

possibly moguće *mogooche*

post (v) poslati poštom
poslatee poshtom

post office pošta *poshta*

postage poštarina
poshtareena

postcard razglednica
razgledneetsa

pot lonac *lonats*

potato krumpir
kroompeer

practice praksa *praksa*

prefer (v) dati prednost
datee prednost, više voljeti
veeshe volyetee

preference prednost
prednost

prescription recept *retsept*

prepare (v) spremiti se
spremeetee se, pripraviti
preepraveetee

present prisutan *preesootan*,
današnji *danashnyee*

  she wasn't present there
  ona nije bila prisutna *ona*
  neeye beela preesootna

  at present times u
  današnje vrijeme *oo*
  danashnye vreeyeme

pretend (v) pretvarati se
pretvaratee se

pretty zgodan *zgodan*

prevent (v) spriječiti
spreeyecheetee

previous prethodni
prethodnee

price cijena *tseeyena*

priest svećenik *svecheneek*

priority prioritet *preeoreetet*

private privatan *preevatan*

probability vjerojatnost
vyeroyatnost

probably vjerojatno
vyeroyatno

procession procesija
protseseeya, povorka *povorka*

produce (v) proizvoditi
proeezvodeetee

product proizvod *proeezvod*

profession profesija *profeseeya*, zvanje *zvanye*

profit profit *profeet*, korist *koreest*

programme program *program*

promise (v) obećati *obechate*

prompt brz *brz*

pronunciation izgovor *eezgovor*

proof dokaz *dokaz*

property vlasništvo *vlasneeshtvo*

propose (v) predložiti *predlozheetee*

proposition prijedlog *preeyedlog*

proprietor vlasnik *vlasneek*

prosciutto pršut *prshoot*

protection zaštita *zashteeta*

protest (v) protestirati *protesteeratee*, prosvjedovati *prosvyedovatee*

provide (v) nabaviti *nabaveetee*, opskrbiti *opskrbeetee*

provision nabava *nabava*

provisional provizoran *proveezoran*, privremen *preevremen*

public javan *yavan*

publication publikacija *poobleekatseeya*

pull (v) vući *voochee*, potezati *potezatee*

puncture probušena guma *probooshena gooma*

punctual točno *tochno*

purchase kupnja *koopnya*

  make purchases kupovati *koopovatee*

pure čist *cheest*

purpose namjera *namyera*, svrha *svrha*

purse novčarka *novcharka*; torbica *torbeetsa*

push (v) gurati *gooratee*

put (v) staviti *staveetee*

  put aside odložiti *odlozheetee*

  put back vratiti *vratiti*

  put down položiti *polozheetee*

  put on obući *oboochee*

  put off svući *svoochee*

Q

qualified kvalificiran *kvaleefeetseeran*, osposobljen *osposoblyen*

quality kvaliteta *kvaleeteta*

quantity količina *koleecheena*

quarrel (v) svađati se *svajatee se*

question pitanje *peetanye*

queue (v) čekati u redu (repu) *chekatee oo redoo (repoo)*

quiet tih *teeh*

quickly brzo *brzo*

quit (v) otići *oteechee*, odustati *odoostatee*

quite sasvim *sasveem*
  quite a few priličan broj *preeleechan broy*

race utrka *ootrka*

radiator radijator *radeeyator*

raft splav *splav*

railway željeznica *zhelyezneetsa*

rain kiša *keesha*

raise (v) povisiti *poveeseetee*, povećati *povechatee*

rare rijedak *reeyedak*

rate tarifa *tareefa*, cijena *tseeyena*
  flat rate paušalna pristojba *paooshalna preestoyba*

rather radije *radeeye*, zapravo *zapravo*

ravine gudura *goodoora*

raw sirov *seerov*

reach (v) doći do *dochee do*

reaction reakcija *reaktseeya*

read (v) čitati *cheetatee*

ready spreman *spreman*, gotov *gotov*

real stvaran *stvaran*; pravi *pravee*
  the real reason pravi razlog *pravee razlog*
  it's real gold to je pravo zlato, *to ye pravo zlato*

realize (v) realizirati *realeezeeratee*, ostvariti *ostvareetee*

really doista *doeesta*, stvarno *stvarno*

reason (think) razum *razoom*; (cause) razlog *razlog*

reasonable razborit *razboreet*, prihvatljiv *preehvatlyeev*

receipt potvrda o primitku *potvrda o preemeetkoo*

receive (v) primiti *preemeetee*

recent nedavan *nedavan*

reception primanje *preemanye*

recognize (v) prepoznati *prepoznatee*

recommend (v) preporučiti *preporoocheetee*

recommendation preporuka *preporooka*

reconsider (v) ponovno razmotriti *ponovno razmotreetee*

record (v) (za)bilježiti *(za)beelyezheetee*

recover (v) dobiti natrag; *dobeetee natrag*; preboljeti *prebolyetee*

he recovered his camera dobio je natrag svoj fotoaparat *dobeeo ye natrag svoj fotoaparat*

she recovered from the flu preboljela je gripu *prebolyela ye greepoo*

red crven *tsrven*

red wine crno vino *tsrno veeno*

reduce (v) sniziti *sneezeetee*, reducirati *redootseeratee*

reduced (price) snižena cijena *sneezhena tseeyena*

reef greben *greben*

sunken reef podvodni greben *podvodnee greben*

refer (v) odnositi se *odnoseetee se*

refill (v) iznova napuniti *eeznova napooneetee*

refresh (v) osvježiti se *osvyezheetee se*

refreshment(s) okrepa *okrepa*; jelo i piće *yelo ee peeche*

refund (v) refundirati *refoondeeratee*, vratiti novac *vrateetee novats*

refund vraćanje novca *vrachanye novtsa*

refuse (v) odbiti *odbeetee*, uskratiti *ooskrateetee*

regain (v) dobiti natrag *dobeetee natrag*

regard pogled *pogled*; pozdrav *pozdrav*

in this regard u tom pogledu *oo tom pogledoo*

with kind regards uz srdačne pozdrave *ooz srdachne pozdrave*

regardless bez obzira na *bez obzeera na*

register (v) upisati (se) *oopeesatee (se)*

regret (v) žaliti *zhaleetee*

regular redovit *redoveet*

rehabilitation rehabilitacija *rehabeeleetatseeya*

reject (v) odbaciti *odbatseetee*

relations rođaci *rojatsee*

relax (v) odmarati se *odmaratee se*

religion religija *releegeeya*, vjera *vyera*

religious religiozan *releegeeozan*, pobožan *pobozhan*

relocation premještanje
premyeshtanye

remain (v) ostati *ostatee*

remark primjedba
preemyedba

make a remark staviti
primjedbu *staveetee*
preemyedboo

remarkable izvanredan
eezvanredan, osobit *osobeet*

remedy lijek *leeyek*

remember (v) pamtiti
pamteetee, sjetiti se
syeteetee se

remote udaljen *oodalyen*

remove (v) ukloniti
ookloneetee maknuti
maknootee

renew (v) obnoviti *obnoveetee*

rent (v) unajmiti *oonaymeetee*,
rentirati *renteeratee*

rent renta *renta*, najamnina
nayamneena

repair (v) popraviti
popraveetee

repair popravak *popravak*

repeat (v) ponoviti
ponoveetee

replace (v) nadomjestiti
nadomyesteetee

replacement zamjena
zamyena

reply (v) odgovoriti
odgovoreetee

report (v) izvijestiti
eezveeyesteetee, prijaviti
preeyaveetee

representative predstavnik
predstavneek

reputation reputacija
repootatseeya

request molba *molba*

make a request zamoliti
zamoleetee

require (v) trebati *trebatee*,
zahtijevati *zahteeyevatee*

requisite rekvizit *rekveezeet*

rescue (v) spašavati
spashavatee, priteći u
pomoć *preetechee*
oo pomoch

reservation rezervacija
rezervatseeya

reserve (v) rezervirati
rezerveeratee

residential stambeni
stambenee

resist (v) odolijevati
odoleeyevatee

resolve (v) riješiti (problem)
reeyesheetee (problem)

resort odmaralište
odmaraleeshte

holiday resort ljetovalište
lyetovaleeshte

seaside resort morsko
kupalište *morsko*
koopaleeshte

respect (v) poštivati *poshteevatee*, cijeniti *ceeyeneetee*

responsible odgovoran *odgovoran*

rest (v) odmarati se *odmaratee se*

restaurant restoran *restoran*

restrict (v) ograničiti *ograneecheetee*

result rezultat *rezooltat*

return (v) vratiti (se) *vrateetee (se)*

return ticket povratna karta *povratna karta*

reverse obratan *obratan*, okrenut *okrenoot*

reward nagrada *nagrada*

ribs rebra *rebra*

rice riža *reezha*

rich bogat *bogat*; obilan *obeelan*

ride (v) jahati *yahatee*; voziti (se) *vozeetee (se)*

  ride a horse jahati konja *yahatee konya*

  ride a bike voziti bicikl *vozeetee beetseekl*

right desno *desno*

  on the right nadesno *nadesno*

  he's right on ima pravo *on eema pravo*

ring (v) pozvoniti *pozvoneetee*

ring (on finger) prsten *prsten*

ripe zreo *zreo*

rise dizanje *deezanye*, uspon *oospon*

risk (v) riskirati *reeskeeratee*

river rijeka *reeyeka*

road cesta *tsesta*

roast pečenka *pechenka*

rock stijena *steeyena*

room soba *soba*

rope konop *konop*, uže *oozhe*

rose ruža *roozha*

rough (sea) buran (more) *booran (more)*

round okrugao *okroogao*

round trip kružno putovanje *kroozhno pootovanye*

row red *red*, niz *neez*

ruin ruševina *roosheveena*

rule propis *propees*, pravilo *praveelo*

run (v) trčati *trchatee*

run out ponestati *ponestatee*

  we've run out of petrol ponestalo nam je benzina *ponestalo nam ye benzeena*

rural seoski *seoskee*

rush žurba *zhoorba*, strka *strka*

sad žalostan *zhalostan*
safe siguran *seegooran*
sail (v) jedriti *yedreetee*
sail jedro *yedro*
sailboat jedrilica *yedreeleetsa*
salad salata *salata*
salami salama *salama*
sale prodaja *prodaya*,
 rasprodaja *rasprodaya*
salt sol *sol*
same isti *eestee*
sandal sandala *sandala*
sand pijesak *peeyesak*
sandwich sendvič *sendveech*
sandy pjeskovit *pyeskoveet*
satisfaction zadovoljstvo
 zadovolystvo
satisfied zadovoljan
 zadovolyan
Saturday subota *soobota*
sauce umak *oomak*
saucepan duboka tava
 dooboka tava
sausage kobasica *kobaseetsa*
save (v) spasiti *spaseetee*
say (v) reći *rechee*, kazati
 kazatee
 so to say tako reći *tako
 rechee*
scare (v) uplašiti *ooplasheetee*
scarf marama *marama*,
 šal *shal*

scene scena *stsena*, prizor
 preezor
scenery vidik *veedeek*
schedule plan *plan*, vozni
 red *voznee red*
 according to schedule
 prema planu *prema planoo*
school škola *shkola*
screwdriver odvijač
 odveeyach
scratch ogrebotina
 ogreboteena
scuba diving ronjenje (s
 bocom) *ronyenye (s botsom)*
sea more *more*
seafood plodovi mora
 plodovee mora
seagull galeb *galeb*
search (v) tražiti *trazheetee*,
 pretraživati *pretrazheevatee*
seashore morska obala
 morska obala
seaside kraj uz more *kray
 ooz more*
 go to the seaside ići na
 more *eechee na more*
sea urchin morski jež
 morskee yezh
seaweed morska alga
 morska alga
season sezona *sezona*,
 godišnje doba *godeeshnye
 doba*
seat sjedalo *syedalo*

seat belt sigurnosni pojas
seegoornosnee poyas
second (time) sekunda
sekoonda; (other) drugi
droogee
second class drugorazredni
droogorazrednee
secretly tajno *tayno*
secure (v) osigurati
oseegooratee
see (v) vidjeti *veedyetee*
  see you doviđenja
  doveejenya
seem (v) izgledati *eezgledatee*
  it seems to me čini mi se
  cheenee mee se
seldom rijetko *reeyetko*
selection izbor *eezbor*
self-service store
  samoposluživanje
  samposloozheevanye
sell (v) prodavati *prodavatee*
send (v) poslati *poslatee*
sentence rečenica *recheneetsa*
separate odvojen
  odvoyen, poseban *poseban*
September rujan *rooyan*;
  septembar *septembar*
serious ozbiljan *ozbeelyan*
serve (v) poslužiti
  posloozheetee, služiti
  sloozheetee
service služba *sloozhba*,
  usluga *ooslooga*

service station servis
  servees
serviette salveta *salveta*,
  ubrus *oobroos*
set (time) određen *odrejen*,
  (price) stalan *stalan*
set menu gotova jela *gotova yela*
settle (v) smjestiti se
  smyesteetee se
seven sedam *sedam*
seventeen sedamnaest
  sedamnaest
seventy sedamdeset
  sedamdeset
several nekoliko *nekoleeko*
severe (strict) strog *strog*;
  (harsh) žestok *zhestok*
shade hladovina *hladoveena*
  sun shade tenda *tenda*
shallow plitak *pleetak*
shampoo šampon *shampon*
shape oblik *obleek*, lik *leek*
  in good shape u dobrom
  stanju *oo dobrom stanyoo*
share (v) dijeliti *deeyeleetee*
shared zajednički
  zayedneechkee
sharp oštar *oshtar*
shave (v) brijati (se)
  breeyatee se
she ona *ona*
sheet plahta *plahta*
shelf polica *poleetsa*

shell (in the sea) školjka *shkolyka*; ljuska *lyooska*

shine (v) sjati *syatee*, svijetliti *sveeyetleetee*

ship brod *brod*

ship yard brodogradilište *brodogradeeleeshte*

shirt košulja *koshoolya*

shoe cipela *tseepela*

shop prodavaonica *prodavaoneetsa*, dućan *doochan*

shopping kupovanje *koopovanye*

shop window izlog *eezlog*

shore obala *obala*

  go on shore iskrcati se *eeskrtsatee se*

  off shore podalje od obale *podalye od obale*

short kratak *kratak*

  short of money bez novaca *bez novatsa*

shortcut prečac *prechats*

shortly uskoro *ooskoro*

shoulder rame *rame*

shout (v) vikati *veekatee*

show (v) pokazati (se) *pokazatee (se)*

  show up pojaviti se *poyaveetee se*

show šou *shooo*, predstava *predstava*

shower tuš *toosh*

take a shower tuširati se *toosheeratee se*

shower (strong rain) pljusak *plyoosak*

shut (v) zatvoriti (se) *zatvoreetee (se)*

shutter roleta *roleta*, prozorski kapak *prozorskee kapak*

shy stidljiv *steedlyeev*

sick bolestan *bolestan*

side strana *strana*

sidewalk pločnik *plochneek*

sight vidik *veedeek*, znamenitost *znameneetost*

sign (v) potpisati *potpeesatee*

signal light žmigavac *zhmeegavats*

signature potpis *potpees*

significant značajan *znachayan*

silent tih *teeh*, šutljiv *shootlyeev*

silk svila *sveela*

silly glup *gloop*, luckast *lootskast*

silver srebro *srebro*

similar sličan *sleechan*

simple jednostavan *yednostavan*

since otada *otada*

  since when? otkada? *otkada*

sincere iskren *eeskren*

sing (v) pjevati *pyevatee*

single jedan jedini *yedan yedeenee*

single (not married) (m) neoženjen *neozhenyen*; (f) neudana *neoodana*

sink sudoper *soodoper*

sister sestra *sestra*

sit (v) sjediti *syedeetee*

sit down sjesti *syestee*

situation situacija *seetooatseeya*

size veličina *veleecheena*

six šest *shest*

sixteen šesnaest *shesnaest*

sixty šezdeset *shezdeset*

skilled stručan *stroochan*

skin koža *kozha*

skirt suknja *sooknya*

souvenir suvenir *sooveneer*

sky nebo *nebo*

sleep (v) spavati *spavatee*

sleeping berth ležaj (na brodu, u vlaku) *lezhay (na brodoo, oo vlakoo)*

slice kriška *kreeshka*, odrezak *odrezak*

slim vitak *veetak*

slimming diet dijeta za mršavljenje *deeyeta za mrshavlyenye*

slipper papuča *papoocha*

slippery sklisko *skleesko*

small malen *malen*

smart (well-dressed) elegantan *elegantan*; (clever) bistar *beestar*

smell (v) (good) mirisati *meereesatee*; (bad) zaudarati *zaoodaratee*

smile (v) smješkati se *smyeshkatee se*

smoked meat dimljeno meso *deemlyeno meso*

smoking pušenje *pooshenye*

smooth gladak *gladak*, (sea) miran *meeran*

snack laki obrok *lakee obrok*, "marenda" *marenda*

snake zmija *zmeeya*

sneaker tenisica *teneeseetsa*

snorkel maska za ronjenje *maska za ronyenye*

snow snijeg *sneeyeg*

so tako *tako*, na ovaj način *na ovay nacheen*

soap sapun *sapoon*

social društven *drooshtven*

socket utičnica *ooteechneetsa*

sofa sofa *sofa*

sofa bed sklopivi krevet *sklopeevee krevet*

soft mekan *mekan*

soft drink bezalkoholno piće *bezalkoholno peeche*

somebody netko *netko*

somehow nekako *nekako*

something nešto *neshto*

sometimes katkada
katkada

son sin *seen*

song pjesma *pyesma*

soon uskoro *ooskoro*

  as soon as što prije, *shto*
  preeye

sore rana *rana*

sorry žalostan *zhalostan*

  I'm sorry žao mi je *zhao*
  mee ye

sort vrsta *vrsta*

sound zvuk *zvook*

  sound-proof zvučno
  izoliran *zvoochno eezoleeran*

soup *yooha*

sour kiseo *keeseo*

sour cream kiselo vrhnje
  keeselo vrhnye

source izvor *eezvor*

south jug *yoog*

southern južni *yoozhnee*

steering wheel volan *volan*

space prostor *prostor*

  there's a lot of space ima
  puno mjesta *eema poono*
  myesta

spark plug svjećica
  svyecheetsa

speak (v) govoriti *govoreetee*

special specijalan *spetsee-*
  yalan, poseban *poseban*

speciality specijalitet
  spetseeyaleetet

specify (v) specificirati
  spetseefeetseeratee

spectacle spektakl *spektakl*,
  prizor *preezor*

speed brzina *brzeena*

speedboat gliser *gleeser*

spell (v) izgovoriti slovo po
  slovo *eezgovoreetee slovo po*
  slovo

spend (v) potrošiti
  potrosheetee, trošiti *trosheetee*

spicy pikantan *peekantan*,
  jako začinjen *yako*
  zacheenyen

spider pauk *paook*

spill (v) proliti *proleetee*

spinach špinat *shpeenat*

splendid divan *deevan*,
  veličanstven *veleechanstven*

spoil (v) pokvariti *pokvareetee*

spoon žlica *zhleetsa*

sport sport *sport*, (fun)
  zabava *zabava*

sport centre sportski centar
  sportskee tsentar

sprain iščašenje *eeshchashenye*

spray sprej *sprey*

spread (food) namaz *namaz*

spring proljeće *prolyeche*

spring (v) skočiti *skocheetee*

springboard odskočna
  daska *odskochna daska*

squall nalet vjetra *nalet*
  vyetra, reful *refool*

square kvadrat *kvadrat*;
(in a town) trg *trg*

staff osoblje *osoblye*

stage pozornica *pozorneetsa*

stain mrlja *mrlya*

stair stepenica *stepeneetsa*,
stuba *stooba*

staircase stubište
stoobeeshte

stamp marka *marka*

stand (v) stajati *stayatee*

stand štand *shtand*

star zvijezda *zveeyezda*

starboard (naut.) desni bok
desnee bok

start (v) krenuti *krenootee*

state država *drzhava*

station stanica *staneetsa*,
postaja *postaya*

stay (v) boraviti *boraveetee*,
ostati *ostatee*

stay boravak *boravak*

steak mesni odrezak *mesny
odrezak*

steal (v) ukrasti *ookrastee*

steep strm *strm*

step korak *korak*

stern (naut) krma *krma*

stew dinstano meso
deenstano meso

steward stjuard *styooard*

stewardess stjuardesa
styooardesa

still tih *teeh*; miran *meeran*

keep still budi miran
boodee meeran

stink (v) zaudarati
zaoodaratee

stomach želudac *zheloodats*

stone kamen *kamen*

stop (v) zaustaviti se
zaoostaveetee se; obustaviti
oboostaveetee

stop at zaustaviti se pred
zaoostaveetee se pred

stop paying that obustaviti
plaćanje (toga) *oboostaveetee plachanye (toga)*

stop (bus) autobusna stanica
aootoboosna staneetsa

store prodavaonica
prodavaoneetsa

storm oluja *olooya*

story priča *preecha*

straight ravno *ravno*

straight ahead samo
ravno *samo ravno*

strange stran *stran*, tuđ *tooj*

strawberry jagoda *yagoda*

stream potok *potok*

street ulica *ooleetsa*

streetcar tramvaj *tramvay*

stroke (med) kap *kap*

strong jak *yak*

student student *stoodent*

study (v) studirati *stoodeeratee*

stuffy zagušljiv *zagooshlyeev*

stupid glup *gloop*

suburb prigradsko naselje *preegradsko naselye*

substitute (v) zamijeniti *zameeyeneetee*

successful uspješan *oospyeshan*

such takav *takav*

suddenly nenadano *nenadano*

sugar šećer *shecher*

suggest (v) sugerirati *soogereeratee*

suitcase kofer *kofer*

suite apartman *apartman*

summer ljeto *lyeto*

sun sunce *soontse*

sunbathe sunčati se *soonchatee se*

sunburn opeklina od sunca *opekleena od soontsa*

Sunday nedjelja *nedyelya*

sunglasses sunčane naočale *soonchane naochale*

sun lotion losion za sunce *loseeon za soontse*

sunscreen zaštitni faktor (za sunčanje) *zashteetnee faktor (za soonchanye)*

sunny sunčan *soonchan*

supper večera *vechera*

support potpora *potpora*

suppose (v) pretpostavljati *pretpostavlyatee*

supposed navodni *navodnee*

surcharge nadoplata *nadoplata*

sure siguran *seegooran*

for sure sigurno *seegoorno*

surfing daskanje *daskanye*, surfanje *soorfanye*

surgery kirurgija *keeroorgeeya*

surname prezime *prezeeme*

surprise (v) iznenaditi *eeznenadeetee*

surround (v) okruživati *okroozheevatee*

suspect (v) (of guilt) sumnjičiti *soomnyeecheetee*; (feeling) slutiti *slooteetee*

sweat (v) znojiti se *znoyeetee se*

sweater vesta *vesta*

sweatshirt zimska majica *zeemska mayeetsa*

sweatsuit trenirka *treneerka*

sweet sladak *sladak*

sweets slatkiši *slatkeeshee*, bomboni *bombonee*

swift brz *brz*

swim (v) plivati *pleevatee*

swimming trunks kupaće gaće *koopache gache*

swimming pool bazen za plivanje *bazen za pleevanye*

swimsuit kupaći kostim *koopachee kosteem*

Swiss chard blitva *bleetva*

table stol *stol*

tablecloth stolnjak *stolnyak*

tag privjesak s imenom *preevyesak s eemenom*

tail light stražnje svjetlo *strazhnye svyetlo*

take (v) uzeti *oozetee*, primiti *preemeetee*, trebati *trebatee*

take back primiti natrag *preemeetee natrag*

take it! uzmite! *oozmeete*

take off uzletjeti *oozletyetee*

take out izvaditi *eezvadeetee*

take care brinuti se *breenootee se*

take part in učestvovati *oochestvovatee*

it takes time za to treba vremena *za to treba vremena*

take photos fotografirati *fotografeeratee*

taken zauzet *zaoozet*; uzet *oozet*

the seat is taken sjedalo je zauzeto *syedalo ye zaoozeto*

talk (v) razgovarati *razgovaratee*

tall visok *veesok*

tank (car) rezervoar *rezervoar*

tap pipa *peepa*

taste (v) kušati *kooshatee*

tasteful ukusan *ookoosan*

tax porez *porez*

tax-free bez poreza *bez poreza*

taxi taksi *taksee*

tea čaj *chay*

teaspoon čajna žlica *chayna zhleetsa*

teach poučavati *pooochavatee*

teacher učitelj *oocheetely*

technician tehničar *tehneechar*

teeth zubi *zoobee*

telephone telefon *telefon/telefon*

telephone booth telefonska govornica *telefonska govorneetsa*

tell (v) reći *rechee*; priopćiti *preeopcheetee*

tell me! reci mi! *retsee mee*

I was told priopćili su mi *preeopcheelee soo mee*

temperature temperatura *temparatoora*

temporary privremen *preevremen*

ten deset *deset*

tenant stanar *stanar*

tender (food) mekan *mekan*

tennis tenis *tenees*

tent šator *shator*

terrace terasa *terasa*

terrible strašan *strashan*

than nego *nego*

thank (v) zahvaliti (se) *zahvaleetee (se)*

thankful zahvalan *zahvalan*

thanks hvala *hvala*

that (m) onaj *onay*, (f) ona *ona*, (n) ono *ono*

theatre kazalište *kazaleeshte*

their njihov *nyeehov*, njihove *nyeehove*, njihova *nyeehova*

them njih *nyeeh*, njima *nyeema*

I saw them vidio sam ih *veedeeo sam eeh*

I gave them dao sam im *dao sam eem*

then tada *tada*, onda *onda*

there tamo *tamo*

therefore zato *zato*, zbog toga *zbog toga*

these (m) ovi *ovee*, (f) ove *ove*, (n) ova *ova*

they (m) oni *onee*, (f) one *one*, (n) ona *ona*

thick gust *goost*

thigh bedro *bedro*

thin tanak *tanak*

thing stvar *stvar*, predmet *predmet*

think (v) misliti *meesleetee*

thirsty žedan *zhedan*

this (m) ovaj *ovay*, (f) ova *ova*, (n) ovo *ovo*

those (m) oni *onee*, (f) one *one*, (n) ona *ona*

three tri *tree*

thirteen trinaest *treenaest*

thirty trideset *treedeset*

throat grlo *grlo*

through skroz *skroz*, kroz *kroz*

throw (v) baciti *batseetee*

throw out izbaciti *eezbatseetee*

thumb palac *palats*

thunderstorm oluja *olooya*

Thursday četvrtak *chetvrtak*

ticket karta *karta*

ticket office prodaja karata *prodaya karata*

tide plima i oseka *pleema ee oseka*

high tide plima *pleema*

low tide oseka *oseka*

tidy uredan *ooredan*

tie (v) zavezati *zavezatee*, povezati *povezatee*

tie kravata *kravata*

tight čvrsto *chvrsto*

tights hulahupke *hoolahoopke*

till do *do*, sve do *sve do*

time vrijeme *vreeyeme*; doba *doba*

at all times u svako doba *oo svako doba*

for a time neko vrijeme *neko vreeyeme*

on time na vrijeme *na vreeyeme*

timetable raspored *raspored*, vozni red *vozni red*

tin konzerva *konzerva*

tiny sitan *seetan*

tip napojnica *napoyneetsa*

tire autoguma *aootogooma*

tired umoran *oomoran*

tissues papirnate maramice *papeernate marameetse*, rupčići *roopcheechee*

to u *u*, do *do*, k *k*

  go to the office ići u ured *eechee oo oored*

  next to me do mene *do mene*

  go to the dentist ići k zubaru *eechee k zoobaroo*

toast prepečenac *prepechenats*

tobacco duhan *doohan*

tobacconist trafika *trafeeka*

today danas *danas*

toe prst na nozi *prst na nozee*

together zajedno *zayedno*

toilet zahod *zahod*, toalet *toalet*, WC *ve ce*

toilet paper toaletni papir *toaletnee papeer*

toll cestarina *tsestareena*

toll gate rampa za naplatu cestarine *rampa za naplatoo tsestareene*

tomorrow sutra *sootra*

tongue jezik *yezeek*

too previše *preveeshe*

  too loud previše glasno *preveeshe glasno*

tools alat *alat*

tooth zub *zoob*

toothache zubobolja *zoobobolya*

top vrh *vrh*

  at the top na vrhu *na vrhoo*

torch (electric) električna baterija *elektreechna batereeya*

total ukupan *ookoopan*

touch (v) dirnuti *deernootee*, taknuti *taknootee*

  don't touch it ne diraj to *ne deeray to*

tough nepopustljiv *nepopoostlyeev*, opasan *opasan*

tour kružno putovanje *kroozhno pootovanye*

tourist turist *tooreest*

tourist office turistički ured *tooreesteechkee oored*

toward(s) prema *prema*

towel ručnik *roochneek*

tower toranj *torany*, kula *koola*

town grad *grad*

  town centre središte grada *sredeeshte grada*

toy igračka *eegrachka*

trade trgovina *trgoveena*, obrt *obrt*

traffic promet *promet*

traffic lights semafor *semafor*

trailer prikolica *preekoleetsa*

tram tramvaj *tramvay*

train vlak *vlak*

transfer prijelaz *preeyelaz*

transit prelaženje *prelazhenye*

translate (v) prevesti *prevestee*

transport prijevoz *preeyevoz*; otpremanje *otpremanye*

travel (v) putovati *pootovatee*

travel agency putnička agencija *pootneechka agentseeya*

traveller putnik *pootneek*

traveller's cheque putnički čekovi *pootneechkee chekovee*

travelling putovanje *pootovanye*

treat (v) postupati s nekim *postoopatee s nekeem*; počastiti *pochasteetee*

she treated me well postupala je sa mnom lijepo *postoopala ye sa mnom leeyepo*

he treated me to a glass

of wine počastio me čašom vina *pochasteeo me chashom veena*

treatment tretman *tretman*, postupak *postoopak*

tree drvo *drvo*

trip izlet *eezlet*, put *poot*

round trip kružno putovanje *kroozhno pootovanye*

take a trip otputovati *otpootovatee*

trouble neprilika *nepreeleeka*, zlo *zlo*

I'm in trouble u neprilici sam *oo nepreeleetsee sam*

trousers hlače *hlache*

true istinit *eesteeneet*

(it's) true istina je *eesteena ye*

trust (v) imati povjerenja *eematee povyerenya*

I trusted him vjerovao sam mu *vyerovao sam mu*

try (v) pokušati *pokooshatee*, iskušati *eeskooshatee*

try on (clothes) isprobati *eesprobatee*

T-shirt majica *mayeetsa*

Tuesday utorak *ootorak*

tunnel tunel *toonel*

turn (v) okrenuti (se) *okrenootee (se)*

turn back okreni (se)
okrenee (se)

turn on the radio upali
radio *oopalee radeeo*

turn off the heating
ugasi grijanje *oogasee
greeyanye*

he turned up pojavio se
poyaveeo se

twice dvaput *dvapoot*

two dva *dva*

twelve dvanaest *dvanaest*

twenty dvadeset *dvadeset*

tyre autoguma *aootogooma*

ugly ružan *roozhan*

umbrella kišobran
keeshobran

unable nesposoban
nesposoban

I'm unable ne mogu
ne mogoo, nisam sposoban
neesam sposoban

unacceptable neprihvatljiv
nepreehvatlyeev

uncertain neizvjestan
neeezvyestan

I'm uncertain nisam
siguran *neesam seegooran*

uncle ujak *ooyak*; stric
streets

unclear nejasan *neyasan*

uncomfortable neudoban
neoodoban

uncomplicated
jednostavan *yednostavan*

unconcious bez svijesti *bez
sveeyestee*

uncountable bezbrojan
bezbroyan

uncovered nepokriven
nepokreeven

undecided neodlučan
neodloochan

under ispod *eespod*, pod *pod*

underground podzeman
podzeman

understand (v) razumjeti
razoomyetee

underwear rublje *rooblye*

undress (v) svući *svoochee*

uneasy nelagodan
nelagodan

unexpected neočekivan
neochekeevan

unfair nepošten *neposhten*,
pristran *preestran*

unfavourable nepovoljan
nepovolyan

unfit neprikladan
nepreekladan, nesposoban
nesposoban

unforgettable nezaboravan
nezaboravan

unfortunate nesretan
nesretan, zlosretan *zlosretan*

unfriendly neprijazan *nepreeyazan*

unhappy nesretan *nesretan*

unhealthy nezdrav *nezdrav*

unimportant nevažan *nevazhan*

unknown nepoznat *nepoznat*

unless osim ako *oseem ako*

unlikely malo vjerojatno *malo vyeroyatno*

unlock (v) otključati *otklyoochatee*

unlucky nesretan *nesretan*

unnecessary nepotreban *nepotreban*

unpack (v) raspakirati *raspakeeratee*

unpleasant neugodan *neoogodan*

unsafe nesiguran *neseegooran*

unsatisfactory neprikladan *nepreekladan*

unsatisfying koji ne zadovoljava *koyee ne zadovolyava*

untie (v) odvezati *odvezatee*

until do *do*, dok ne *dok ne*

until Friday do petka *do petka*

until you go away dok ne odeš *dok ne odesh*

untrue lažan *lazhan*

unusual neobičan *neobeechan*

unwell bolestan *bolestan*

up gore *gore*, sve do *sve do*

she's up in her room ona je gore u svojoj sobi *ona ye gore oo svoyoy sobee*

up to yesterday sve do jučer *sve do yoocher*

upset (v) uznemiriti (se) *ooznemeereetee (se)*

upset uzrujan *oozrooyan*

he was very upset on se jako uzrujao *on se yako oozrooyao*

upstairs na gornjem katu *na gornyem katoo*

urgent hitan *heetan*

us nas *nas*

to us nama *nama*

usage običaj *obeechay*

use (v) upotrijebiti *oopotree-yebeetee*, rabiti *rabeetee*

used to navikut *naveeknoot*

useful koristan *koreestan*

usual običan *obeechan*

vacant prazan *prazan*, slobodan *slobodan*

vacation godišnji odmor *godeeshnyee odmor*

valid pravomoćan *pravomochan*, koji vrijedi *koyee vreeyedee*

valley dolina *doleena*
valuable dragocjen *dragotsyen*
van kombi *kombee*
variety raznolikost
raznoleekost
vase vaza *vaza*
veal teletina *teleteena*
vegetable povrće *povrche*
vegeterian (m)
vegeterijanac *vegetereeyanats*
vegeterian (f)
vegeterijanka *vegetereeyanka*
vehicle vozilo *vozeelo*
very vrlo *vrlo*, jako *yako*
  very good vrlo dobro *vrlo
  dobro*
  very warm jako toplo
  yako toplo
video video *veedeo*
view pogled *pogled*
village selo *selo*
vinegar ocat *otsat*
vineyard vinograd *veenograd*
violent nasilan *naseelan*
visa viza *veeza*
visible vidljiv *veedlyeev*
visit (v) posjetiti *posyeteetee*
visitor posjetitelj *posyeteetely*
voice glas *glas*
vomitting povraćanje
  povrachanye
voyage plovidba *ploveedba*
voucher vaučer *vaoocher*

wait (v) čekati *chekatee*
waiter konobar *konobar*
waitress konobarica
  konobareetsa
wake (up) (v) probuditi (se)
  proboodeetee (se)
walk (v) hodati *hodatee*;
  šetati *shetatee*
walk hod *hod*; šetnja *shetnya*
  go for a walk ići u šetnju
  eechee oo shetnyoo
wall zid *zeed*
wallet novčarka *novcharka*,
  lisnica *leesneetsa*
walnut orah *orah*
wander (v) lutati *lootatee*
want (v) željeti *zhelyetee*,
  htjeti *htyetee*
  I want a glass of wine
  želim čašu vina *zheleem
  chashoo veena*
  I want him to come here
  hoću da on dođe ovamo
  hochoo da on doje ovamo
war rat *rat*
wardrobe ormar za odjeću
  ormar za odyechoo
warm topao *topao*; ugrijan
  oogreeyan
warning opomena *opomena*
was, (he) (on) je bio *(on)
  ye beeo*

was, (she) (ona) je bila *(ona) ye **beela***

was, (it) (ono) je bilo *(ono) ye beelo*

wash (v) prati (se) *pratee (se)*

wasp osa *osa*

watch (v) motriti *motreetee*; gledati *gledatee*

watch ručni sat *roochnee sat*

  it's 2 by my watch na mojem je satu 2 *na moyem ye satoo dva*

watchmaker urar *oorar*

water voda *voda*

waterfall slap *slap*

watermelon lubenica *loobeneetsa*

waterskiing skijanje na vodi *skeeyanye na vodee*

wave val *val*

way put *poot*; način *nacheen*

  I can't find the way to ne mogu naći put za *ne mogoo nachee poot za*

  in this way na taj način *na tay nacheen*

we mi *mee*

weak slab *slab*

wear (v) (clothes) nositi (odjeću) *noseetee (odyechoo)*

weather vrijeme *vreeyeme*

  fair weather lijepo vrijeme *leeyepo vreeyeme*

weather forecast prognoza vremena *prognoza vremena*

Wednesday srijeda *sreeyeda*

week tjedan *tyedan*

weekend vikend *veekend*

weekly tjedno *tyedno*

weight težina *tezheena*

welcome dobrodošao *dobrodoshao*

well dobro *dobro*

  he swims well dobro pliva *dobro pleeva*

well zdrav *zdrav*

  I'm well zdrav sam *zdrav sam*

were (we) (mi) smo bili/bile *(mee) smo beelee/beele*

were, (you) (vi) ste bili/bile *(vee) ste beelee/beele*

were, (they) (oni, one, ona) su bili/bile/bila *(onee, one, ona) su beelee/beele/beela*

were, (familiar you) (ti) si bio/bila *tee see beeo/beela*

west zapad *zapad*

wet mokar *mokar*

what što *shto*

whatever bilo što *beelo shto*

wheel kotač *kotach*

when kada *kada*

where gdje *gdye*

which koji *koyee*

while časak *chasak*

in a little while za časak
za chasak, za tren *za tren*
while dok *dok*
while you were out dok
si bio vani *dok see beeo
vanee*
white bijel *beeyel*
white wine bijelo vino
beeyelo veeno
who tko *tko*
whole cio *tseeo*
whole wheat bread kruh
od integralnog brašna
*krooh od eentegralnog
brashna*
why zašto *zashto*
wide širok *sheerok*
widow udovica *oodoveetsa*
widower udovac *oodovats*
wife supruga *sooprooga*,
žena *zhena*
wild divlji *deevlyee*
will (v) htjeti *htyetee*, željeti
zhelyetee
willing voljan *volyan*
wind vjetar *vyetar*
window prozor *prozor*
windscreen vjetrobran
vyetrobran
windshield vjetrobran
vyetrobran
windsurfing surfanje na
vjetru *soorfanye na
vyetroo*, daskanje *daskanye*

windsurfing sail board
daska za jedrenje *daska za
yedrenye*
wine vino *veeno*
winter zima *zeema*
wiper (car) brisač
breesach
wire žica *zheetsa*
wish (v) željeti *zhelyetee*
with s *s*; kod *kod*
with my sister s mojom
sestrom *s moyom sestrom*
I've no money with me
nemam novaca kod sebe
nemam novatsa kod sebe
without bez *bez*
witness svjedok *svyedok*
wonder (v) čuditi se
choodeetee se; pitati se
peetatee se
**I wonder at his
behaviour** čudim se
njegovom ponašanju
*choodeem se nyegovom
ponashanyoo*
I wonder who she is
pitam se tko je ona *peetam
se tko ye ona*
wonderful divan *deevan*
woman žena *zhena*
women žene *zhene*
wood drvo *drvo*
wool vuna *voona*
word riječ *reeyech*

work (v) raditi *radeetee*

work rad *rad*, posao *posao*,
djelo *dyelo*

**I'm exhausted by my
work** moj rad/posao me je
iscrpio *moy rad/posao me
ye eestsrpeeo*

**his work made him
famous** njegovo ga je djelo
proslavilo *nyegovo ga ye
dyelo proslaveelo*

workshop radionica
radeeoneetsa

world svijet *sveeyet*

worried zabrinut *zabreenoot*

worry (v) brinuti (se)
breenootee (se)

worse gori *goree*

worst najgori *naygoree*

worthless bezvrijedan
bezvreeyedan

wrap up zamotati *zamotatee*

wrist zglavak *zglavak*

wrist band remen za ručni
sat *remen za roochnee sat*,
narukvica *narookveetsa*

write (v) pisati *peesatee*

write down zapisati
zapeesatee

wrong kriv *kreev*,
neispravan *neeespravan*

this is the wrong way to
je krivi put *to ye kreevee
poot*

x-ray rentgen *rentgen*

year godina *godeena*

yellow žut *zhoot*

yesterday jučer *yoocher*

yes da *da*

you (familiar) ti *tee*;
(formal) vi *vee*

yoghurt jogurt *yogoort*

young mlad *mlad*

your (familiar) tvoj *tvoy*;
(formal) vaš *vash*

youth mladež *mladezh*

zoo zoološki vrt *zooloshkee
vrt*

zucchini tikvice *teekveetse*

A

adresa address
agencija agency
  turistička agencija travel
  agency
ako if
aktualan actual
akumulator (car) battery
alat tools
alkohol alcohol
aleja tree-lined walk
alga algae
  morske alge seaweed
alergičan allergic
alergija (med.) allergy
ambasada embassy
ambulanta consulting
  room, surgery, doctor's
  office
američki American
Amerika America
Amerikanac (m)
  American
Amerikanka (f) American
ananas pineapple
angina (med.) tonsillitis
aranžman arrangement
Australija Australia
Australac (m) Australian
Australka (f) Australian
australski Australian
auto car
autobus bus, coach

autobusni kolodvor bus
  station
**autobusna/tramvajska
  stanica** bus/tram stop
autocesta highway
autokarta road-map
autoguma tyre, tire
  pukla mi je guma
  I've a flat tyre
automobil automobile
autopraonica carwash

B

baciti (v) throw (away),
  discard
  baciti sidro (v) cast anchor
badem almond
bakalar (fish) cod
bakreni made of copper
balkon balcony
balet ballet
banana banana
banka bank
bankomat bank machine
barbun (fish) red mullet
baterija battery
bazen pool
beba doll
benzin petrol, gasoline
  normalni regular
  super premium, super
  bezolovni lead-free
  dizel diesel

benzinska stanica petrol station, gas(oline) station
beskoristan useless
besplatan free of charge
besplatan ulaz free admission
bez without
bezalkoholni napici non-alcoholic drinks, soft drinks
bicikl bicycle
voziti se biciklom ride a bicycle
bife pub, snack-bar
bijel white
bio/bila sam I was
bio/bila si (informal) you were
bili/bile smo we were
bili/bile/bila ste you were
bili /bile/bila su they were
birati (v) choose
bistar clear (sky); clever
biti (v) be
bježati (v) run
blagajna check-out counter
blagajna za putne karte booking-office
blagajna za ulaznice ticket-office, box-office
blagdan holiday
blagovaonica dining room
blatobran wing, fender
blijed pale

blitva Swiss chard
blizu near, by
bluza blouse
boca bottle
Bog God
bogat rich
boja colour
bojati se (v) be afraid
jako se bojim I'm scared
bojenje (kose) (hair) colouring
bok (naut.) side
desni bok broda starboard
lijevi bok broda port side
bokobran (naut) fender
bolan painful
bolestan sick, ill
bolnica hospital
bolničarka nurse
bolje better
boljeti (v) feel pain, hurt
bombon sweet, candy
boraviti (v) stay (at), reside
boravak stay
stalni boravak residence
borovnica blueberry
Božić Christmas
brašno flour
brat brother
brava lock
brdo hill, mountain
breskva peach
brijačnica barber's (shop)
brijati se (v) shave

brinuti se (v) worry; take care

 ne brini se don't worry

brisač (car) wiper

Britanija Britain

britanski British

brod ship, boat

brodet fish stew

brodogradilište shipyard

broj number, (clothes and shoes) size

broš brooch

brošura brochure

brz fast, quick, swift

brzina speed

 ograničena brzina speed limit

brzo quickly, rapidly

bučan noisy, loud

budilica alarm-clock

buditi (v) wake(up)

bura north-eastern wind

buzara cooked shellfish with wine, garlic and parsley

carina customs

 prijaviti na carini (v) declare

carinik customs officer

carinske pristojbe customs duties

carinski pregled customs control

centar centre

 centar grada centre of town/city

centrala head office

 centrala (telephoning) operator

cesta road

 glavna cesta major/main road

cestarina toll

 naplatno mjesto za cestarinu toll-gate

cigareta cigarette

cijel whole, entire

cijena price

cilj puta destination

cipal (fish) grey mullet

cipela shoe

cjenkati se (v) bargain (for)

cjenik price list

crkva church

crn black

crta line

crven red

curiti, kapati (v) flow; drip

cvijet flower

cvjetača cauliflower

cvjećarnica flower shop

Č

čaj tea
čajnik teapot
čamac boat
čarape stockings
  sokne socks
  hulahupke tights, pantyhose
čaroban charming, fascinating
čas(ak) moment
  samo časak just a moment
časopis magazine
častiti (v) treat
  ja častim it's my treat
čaša glass
ček cheque
čekaonica waiting room
čekaonica u zračnoj luci (airport) departure lounge
čekati (v) wait
čestitati (v) congratulate
  čestitam my congratulatios
često often, frequently
češalj comb
češljati (se) (v) comb
češnjak garlic
četka brush
četkica za zube toothbrush
četiri four
četrdeset forty

četrnaest fourteen
četvrt quarter
četvrtak Thursday
čiji whose
čim as soon as
činiti (v) do, make
činiti se (v) seem, appear
  čini mi se it seems to me
činjenica fact
čipka lace
čist clean
čistiti (v) clean up; cleanse
čitati (v) read
čizma boot
član member
čokolada chocolate
čovjek man
čuditi se (v) wonder, be astonished
čudo miracle
čudan odd, unusual
čuti (v) hear
čuvar guard, security guard
čuvati (v) protect
čuven famous
čvor knot

Ć

će (he/she/it; they) will
ćeš/ćete (you) will
ćemo (we) shall, will
ćete (you)

ćevapčići grilled minced meat

ću (I) shall, will

D

da yes

dagnja mussel

dagnje na buzaru mussels cooked with wine, garlic and parsley

dalek far (off), distant

kako daleko how far

Dalmacija Dalmatia

Dalmatinac (m) Dalmatian

Dalmatinka (f) Dalmatian

dalmatinski Dalmatian

daljina distance

dan day

danas today

dar present

daska board

daska za jedrenje winsurfing/sail board

dati (v) give

datum date

davni ancient

debeo fat

dečko (momak) young man

deka (pokrivač) blanket

dekagram (deka) decagram

10 deka appr. a quarter (pound)

deset ten

desni right

desno on (to) the right

desert sweet (course), dessert

deterdžent detergent

devedeset ninety

devet nine

devetnaest nineteen

devize foreign exchange

dezodorans deodorant

dežuran on duty

dijeliti (napola) (v) halve; share

dijabetes (med) diabetes

dijamant diamond

dijeta diet

dijete child

dimljeno meso smoked meat

dinstati (v) stew, braise, sautee

dinja melon, cantaloupe

dio part

rezervni dio spare part

dirati (v) touch

direktan direct

direktor manager, director

dirigent (mus.) conductor

disanje breathing

disati (v) breathe

dizel diesel

disko disco

diskoteka discotheque

divan wonderful, magnificent

diviti se (v) admire
dizalo lift, elevator
djeca chidren
dječak (young) boy
djed grandfather
djetešce baby
djevojčica little girl
djevojka girl, young
  woman; sweetheart
dnevna soba living room
do till, until; to
  do nedjelje till Sunday
  je li daleko do plaže is it
  far to the beach
doba time(s); age
  godišnje doba season
dobar good
dobar dan good afternoon
dobiti (v) get, receive
dobra večer good evening
dobro well
dobrodošli welcome
dobro jutro good morning
doček reception; welcome
dočekati (v) receive, meet
doći (v) come; arrive; show up
  doći po (nekoga) pick up
dodatak supplement
dodati (v) add
dodijati (v) bother, annoy
događaj event, happening
dogoditi se (v) happen
  što se dogodilo what
  happened

dogovarati se (v) make
  arrangements
dok dock
dokaz proof
dokle how long
doktor doctor
dokument document
dolar dollar
dolazak arrival
dolaziti (v) arrive
doletjeti (v) come by plane
dolina valley
dolje below; down
dom home
domjenak party
domovina native country,
  homeland
donijeti (v) bring
dopisivanje correspondence
doplata extra/additional
  payment; cover charge
doplatiti (v) pay extra
dopodne in the morning
dopratiti (v) accompany,
  come along with
dopust leave
  na dopustu on leave
dopustiti (v) allow, permit
doputovati (u) arrive (in, at)
doručak breakfast
doručkovati (v) have
  breakfast
dosta enough
dostava delivery

dovesti (v) bring (along)
doviđenja goodbye,
see you, so long
dovoljan sufficient
dovršiti (v) finish, conclude
dozvola license, permission
dozvoliti (v) permit, allow
drag dear, nice
  drago mi je I'm
  glad/pleased
dražestan charming, lovely
drogerija chemist's (shop),
drugstore
drugi second
drukčiji different,
in another manner
društvo society, company
drven made of wood,
wooden
drvo tree
držati (v) hold
država country, state
državljanin citizen
dućan shop, store
dubok deep
dug long
dugo a long time
  kako dugo how long
dužnost duty
dva two
dvadeset twenty
dvanaest twelve
dvokrevetna soba double
room

dvorac castle
dvorana hall
  plesna dvorana
ballroom, dance hall

džem jam
džemper pullover, sweater
džep pocket
džin gin

ekran screen; visual display
ekskurzija excursion
ekspeditivan efficient
eksponaža exposure
ekspresni express
elegantan elegant, smart
električna struja electric
current, power
Engleska England
engleski English
Engleskinja (f) English
Englez (m) English
espresso espresso coffee
euro euro
euroček eurocheque,
eurocheck
Europa Europe
europski European
eventualan possible
evidencija records, files

F

faks fax
far headlight
farmaceut pharmacist
fenirati (v) blow-dry (hair)
ferije holidays, vacation
fileki tripes
film film, picture, movie
fin fine, delicate, exquisite
  to je fina osoba nice,
  decent person
  to je fina izradba it's an
  exquisite piece of work
  ja sam dobro I'm fine
fitnes fitness
flaster bandage
fleš flash
formular form
  ispuniti formular fill (in,
  up) a form
fotoaparat camera
fotografija photography
frigati (v) fry
fritule (sweet) fritters
fotokopija photocopy
frizer hair stylist, hairdresser
frizura hairstyle, hair-do

 G

gaće pants, underpants
gaćice panties
galeb seagull
galerija gallery
garancija guarantee
garderoba za kapute
  cloak-room, check-room
garderoba za prtljagu
  luggage room
gdje where
glačalo, pegla iron
glačati (v) iron, press
gladak smooth
gladan hungry
glasan loud
glasovir piano
glasovit famous
glava head
glavni main, chief,
  principal
glavobolja headache
glazba music
gledati (v) look at
gležanj ankle
gliser speed boat
glumac actor
glumica actress
glumiti (v) act, play
gljiva mushroom
godina year
godišnji odmor holidays,
  vacation

gora mountain
gorak bitter
gore above, high up
gore worse
  sve gore i gore worse and worse
gornji upper, top
gospodin Sir, Mr
gospođica Miss
gospođa Madam, Mrs
gost guest
gostionica inn, pub
gotov finished, done
gotovina cash
govedina beef
  kuhana govedina boiled beef
  pečena govedina roast beef
  goveđi bubrežnjak sirloin, tenderloin steak
  goveđi odrezak beefsteak
  ramstek rump-steak
govoriti (v) speak
grad town, city
gradsko središte town centre
gradele grill
  riba na gradele grilled fish
građanin citizen
građevina building
grah beans
granica border, frontier
grašak peas

grijanje heating
grdobina (fish) angler, frog fish
grlo throat
grlobolja sore throat
groznica fever
grožđe grapes, talk
grudnjak bra; brassiere
gubiti (v) lose
guma na kotaču tyre, tire
  probušila mi se guma I've a flat tyre
  žvakaća guma chewing gum
gumb button
gust thick
gužva crowd

halo hello
haljina dress
hauba (car) bonnet, hood
hidrogliser hydrofoil
hitan urgent
hitna pomoć emergency
hitno quickly, fast
hlače trousers, pants
hladno cold, chilly
hladnjak fridge
hladovina shade
hobotnica octopus
  salata od hobotnice octopus salad

hodati (v) walk, go
hodnik passage, corridor
hotel hotel
hren horseradish
hrana food, fare
hrenovka frankfurter
hrenovka u pecivu hot dog
hridina cliff
Hrvat (m) Croatian
Hrvatica (f) Croatian
Hrvatska Croatia
hrvatski Croatian
htjeti will, want
  hoću I will
  hoćeš li will you
  hoćemo li shall we
hulahupke tights
hvala thanks
  hvala lijepa thanks a lot
hvaliti praise

i and
ići (v) go, walk
idući next, following
igla needle
igra game, play
igračka toy
igralište playground, sports ground
igrati se (v) play, gamble
ikada ever

ikakav any
ili or
imati (v) have, possess
ime name
imenik (name) list, register
imitacija imitation
informacija information
  informacijski ured enquiry office, information bureau
informirati se (v) make inquiries, find out
inozemni foreign
inozemstvo foreign country
interesantan interesting
invalid disabled person, invalid
investicija investment
inženjer engineer
injekcija injection
Irac (m) Irish
Irkinja (f) Irish
Irska Ireland
irski Irish
iseliti se (v) move out
iskaznica identity card
iskrcati se (v) land, disembark
iskrcavanje landing, disembarkation
iskustvo experience
ispeći (v) bake, roast, grill, broil
isporučiti (v) deliver

isprava document, identification papers
isprazniti (v) clear out
  isprazniti sobu check out of the room
ispred before, in front
ispričati se (v) apologize, excuse oneself
isprobati (v) try out, test; try on
ispržiti (v) fry
ispuniti fill out, fill up
ispušna cijev (car) exhaust-pipe, muffler
istinit true
istjecati (v) run out, expire
  rok trajanja expiry date
isto the same
istok east
išta anything
itko anyone
iz from
iza behind
izabrati (v) choose
izaći (v) come out, go out
izbor choice
izdatak expense
izdržati stand up, endure
izgubiti (v) lose
izgubljen lost, missing
izlaz exit
  izlaz za nuždu emergency exit

izlet excursion, trip
izletnički autobus tour bus
izletnički brod pleasure boat
iznajmiti (v) let, lease, rent
iznajmljivanje rental, leasing
iznijeti (v) bring (take, carry) out
iznos amount
izrađen made, produced
izvan out of
izvana from (the) outside
izvezeno embroidered
izvrsno excellent
izvoljeti (v) please, be pleased to
  izvolite (offering food) help yourself, have some

ja I
jabuka apple
  pita od jabuka apple pie
  savijača od jabuka apple strudel
jabukov sok apple juice
Jadransko more the Adriatic Sea
jagoda strawberry
jahati ride
jahta yacht

jaje egg
  meko/tvrdo kuhano jaje
  soft/hard boiled egg
  kajgana scrambled eggs
  jaje na oko fried egg
  šunka s jajima ham and
  eggs
jak strong
jako very, extremely
  jako dobro very good
jakna jacket
janjetina lamb's meat
  pečena janjetina roast
  lamb
  janjeći kotleti na žaru
  grilled lamb cutlets
  janjetina na ražnju lamb
  on the spit
jasno clearly, obviously
jastog (shellfish) lobster
jastuk pillow
javan public
je/je li is/is it
jedan one
jedanaest eleven
jedanput once
jedino only
jednokrevetna soba single
  room
jednostavan simple
jedrenje sailing
jedrenje na dasci
  windsurfing
jedrilica sailboat

jedriličarski klub yachting
  club
jedro sail
jedva hardly
jeftin cheap, inexpensive
jelo food, fare
jelovnik menu
jer because
jesam I am
jesen autumn, fall
jesi you are
jesmo we are
jeste you are
jesti (v) eat
jesu they are
jezero lake
jezik tongue
jezik language
jogurt yoghurt
još malo a little more
još ne not yet
jučer yesterday
jug south
jugo south wind
juha soup
  bistra juha clear soup,
  consomme
  gusta juha thick soup
  mesna juha s povrćem
  meat and vegetable soup
  riblja juha fish soup
jutro morning
  dobro jutro good morning

k towards, to
kabina cabin
kačkati, heklati (v) crochet
kad when
kada bathtub
kafe-bar coffee/espresso bar
kafić licensed coffee/espresso bar
kakao cocoa
kakav what (a), what kind/sort of
kako how, in what manner
kalendar calendar
kamen stone, rock
kamera camera
kamion lorry, truck
kamo where
kamp campsite
kampiranje camping
kamp-kućica caravan, motor-home
kamp-prikolica camp trailer
Kanada Canada
kanadski Canadian
Kanađanin (m) Canadian
Kanađanka (f) Canadian
kanu canoe
kao as, like
kapa hat, cap
kapetanija (lučka) harbour master's office

kaput coat
karavan trailer
karmenadl, kotlet chop, cutlet
karta card
　putna karta ticket
kasnije later
kasno late
kasniti (v) be late, be delayed
kašalj (med) cough
kat floor, storey
katedrala cathedral
katkada sometimes
katolik catholic
kaucija deposit
kava coffee
kavana café, coffee-house
kazalište theatre
kazati (v) say, tell
kazna penalty
kćerka daughter
keks biscuit
keramika ceramics
kesten chesnut
kilogram kilogram
kineski Chinese
kikiriki peanuts
kino cinema, movie theatre
kip statue
kiseo sour
kiseli kupus sauerkraut
kiša rain
kišobran umbrella

klasa class
klijent client
klima climate
klimatizacija air-conditioning
klimatski uređaj air-conditioner
klinika clinical hospital
klizaljka skate
klub club
klupa bench
ključ key
knjiga book
knjižara bookshop
kobasica sausage
kočnica brake
kod at, by, with
kofer suitcase
kraći shorter
koji who, what, which
kokos coconut
kola cart, waggon
kolač cake
koliko how much (many)
kolovoz August
koljeno knee
komad piece, slice
komadić small piece
komarac mosquito
kombi (car) van
komu to whom
komfor comfort
komotan comfortable
kompjutor computer

kompliciran complicated
kompliment compliment
kompot stewed fruit
konačan final
koncert concert
konoba wine-cellar, tavern
konobar waiter
konobarica waitress
konop cord, line, rope
konto account
konzerva tin, can
konzulat consulate
konj horse
konjak cognac
korak step
korist benefit, advantage
koristan useful
kosa hair
kost bone
košara basket
koštati (v) cost
  koliko košta how much is it
košulja shirt
kotač wheel
kotlet cutlet
kovčeg chest, box
koverta envelope
koža skin, (material) leather
kožnat made of leather
krađa theft
krafna doughnut
kraj end, conclusion
kralješnica spine

krasan splendid, magnificent
krastavac cucumber
krasti (v) steal
kratak short
kravata tie
kredit credit
kreditna kartica credit card
krema cream dessert
krema za lice facial cream
kremšnita custard slice
krenuti start, move
krevet bed
krigla beer mug
kristal crystal
kriv guilty, wrong
krma (naut.) stern
kroz through
krstarenje cruising, cruise
kruh bread
  bijeli white bread
  crni brown bread
  integralni whole-wheat bread
  kukuruzni corn bread
  raženi rye bread
  domaći home-made bread
krumpir potato
  pire mashed potatoes
  kuhani boiled potatoes
  pečeni baked potatoes
  prženi fried potatoes
  restani sauteed potatoes
krupan large, big

kruška pear
kružno putovanje tour
krv blood
krvni tlak blood pressure
kuća house
  kod kuće at home
kućni domestic
kud(a) which way, where
kuglica sladoleda a scoop of ice cream
kuglana bowling-alley
kuhati (v) cook
kuhano (meso) boiled (meat)
kuhinja kitchen
  čajna kuhinja kitchenette
kulen paprika flavored salami
kultura culture
kuna kuna
kupalište bathing-place
kupanje bathing
kupaonica bathroom
kupiti (v) buy, purchase
kupovina shopping
kupus cabbage
kušati (v) taste
kutija box
kvaka door-handle
kvaliteta quality
kvalitetan high-grade
kvar breakdown, failure
kvariti (v) spoil

L

lađa ship, boat
lagan light
lak za kosu hair spray
lak za nokte nail polish
lakat elbow
lako easily
lakše more easily
laku noć good night
lanac chain
lanen made of linen
lani last year
lavanda lavender
lažan false, untrue
leća lens
  kontaktne leće contact
  lenses
leći (v) lie down
led ice
leden ice-cold
ledeni čaj ice-tea
leđa (body) back
lešada boiled fish/meat
  lešada od oslića boiled hake
ležaljka deck chair
lice face
lift elevator
lignja squid
  lignje na žaru grilled
  squids
  pržene lignje squid fritters
liječenje medical treatment
liječnik physician, doctor
lijek medicine, medication
lijen lazy
lijep beautiful, attractive
lijevi left
lijevo on the left
limun lemon
limunada lemonade
linija line
lipanj June
list leaf; (fish) sole
lisnica wallet, purse
listopad October
lomiti (v) break
lonac pot
lopov thief
lopta ball
losion lotion
loš bad
loše not well, badly
lovor laurel
loza vine
lozovača grape brandy
lubin (fish) sea bass
lučica little port, marina
luk onion
luka harbour
lupati (v) knock, bang,
  beat
lutati (v) wander
lutka doll

ljekarna pharmacy
ljekarnik pharmacist, chemist
lješnjak hazelnut
ljeto summer
ljetovalište summer resort
ljetovati (v) spend summer
ljubav love
ljubazan kind, nice
ljubičast purple
ljubimac favourite, pet
 kućni ljubimci pets
ljubiti (se) (v) kiss
ljudi people
ljut angry; (taste) hot, spicy
ljutiti se (v) be angry/cross
 nemoj se ljutiti don't be angry

mačka cat
maestral landward breeze
magistrala main (trunk) road
 Jadranska magistrala Adriatic Highway
magla fog
mahuna French beans, green beans
majica T-shirt
majka mother

majoneza mayonnaise
maknuti (v) move, remove
makovnjača poppyseed cake
malen small, little
malina raspberry
malo a little
mamac bait
mandarinka tangerine
margarin margarine
manje less
marina (harbour) marina
marelica apricot
marka stamp, postage stamp
marljiv hard-working
maslac butter
maslina olive
maslinovo ulje olive oil
masnoća fat, grease
 s malo masnoće low-fat
med honey
medicinski medical
meduza jelly-fish
međugradski telefonski razgovor long-distance call
međunarodni international
mehaničar mechanic, repairman
mek soft, tender
mene, me me
 za mene for me
meni, mi to me

daj mi to give it to me
mesnica butcher's (shop)
meso meat
  kuhano (pečeno) meso
  boiled (roast) meat
  kosano meso minced
  meat
  meso na žaru grilled meat
  suho (dimljeno) meso
  smoked meat
metar meter
mi we
micati (v) move, stir
mijenjati change
milijun million
mineralna voda mineral
  water
  negazirana mineralna
  voda non-carbonated
  mineral water
mir peace
miran still, calm, peaceful
miris smell
mirovati (v) rest
misa mass
misao thought
misliti (v) think, reason
mjehur blister
mjenjačnica exchange
  office
mjera measure
mjesec the moon, month
mjesto place, spot
mlad young

mlijeko milk
mlinci side dish made of
  fat-free dough
mnogi many
mnogo much, a lot of
mobitel cellular phone
moći be able, can
  mogu li can I
modar dark/deep blue
moguće possibly
  ako je moguće if possible
moj my
mokar wet
molba request
moliti (v) ask, request, beg
  molim vas recite mi tell
  me please
  molim (repeat it please)
  pardon, excuse me
momak young man, boy;
  steady boy-friend
morati (v) have to, must
more sea
morski jež sea-urchin
most bridge
motel motel
motocikl motorcycle
motociklist motorcyclist
motor engine
motriti (v) watch
možda perhaps
mrak dark, darkness
mreža net
mrlja stain

mršav thin
mrtav dead
muzej museum
muž husband, man

na on
nabaviti (v) obtain, get
način manner, way
načiniti (v) make, produce
naći (v) find
nadati se (v) hope
nadesno to the right
nadjeven stuffed
naknada compensation
nadoplatiti (v) make an
  additional payment
nagovoriti (v) persuade,
  talk into
nagrada reward
najam hire, lease
najamnina rent, rental (fee)
najava announcement
najbliži the nearest
najbolji the best
najčešći the most
  frequent
najednom suddenly
najnoviji the latest, the
  most recent
nakit jewellery
nakon after
nalaziti se (v) find oneself

gdje se nalazi ... where
  is ...
nalijevo to the left
nam(a) to us
namirnice food, victuals
namjeravati (v) intend, plan
namještenje employment,
  job
naočale glasses, spectacles
naočale za sunce
  sunglasses
napadaj (med) seizure, attack
napadnut attacked
napisati (v) write (down)
naplatiti charge
napojnica tip
napor effort
napraviti (v) make, produce
napredak progress
naprijed forward, ahead
naprtnjača knapsack,
  backpack
napuniti (v) fill up
naranča orange
narančast (colour) orange
narezan sliced
narezati (v) cut into, slice up
naročito specially,
  particularly
narod the people, nation
naručiti (v) order
narudžba order
  po narudžbi to order
narukvica bracelet

nas us
naslonjač armchair, easy chair
nastradati be/get hurt, meet with an accident
nasuprot opposite; across the road
naš our
natrag back, backwards
naušnice earrings
navečer in the evening
naviknuti se (v) get/become used
navrijeme on time
nazdravlje cheers
nazvati (v) phone, give a call
  nazovi me give me a call
ne no
neće he/she/they will not
nećemo we will not
nećeš you will not
neću I will not, I shall not
nedaleko not far off/away
nedjelja Sunday
negaziran non-carbonated
negdje somewhere
nego than
neispravan faulty, out of order
nekako somehow
nekoliko a few, some
nemastan fat-free, low-fat
nema there is/are not
nemati (v) have not, lack

nemoguće impossible
nemoj do not, don't
neobičan unusual
neoženjen (m) unmarried, single
nepokretan unable to move, bed-ridden
nepopunjen vacant
nepovjerenje distrust
nepoznat unknown
nepozvan uninvited
nepravilan irregular
neprekidan continual
neprijazan unfriendly
neprilika trouble; difficulty
nepromočiv waterproof
nepušač nonsmoker
nerashlađen uncooled, unchilled
nerazumljiv hard to understand
nered mess, untidiness
nesporazum misunderstanding
nesreća bad luck, misfortune
  prometna nesreća traffic accident
nesretan unhappy
nesvijest faint, loss of consciousness
nešto something
netko somebody
neugodan unpleasant
nezgoda accident

nije he/she/it is not
nikad never
nisam I am not
nisi/niste you are not
nismo we are not
nisu they are not
ništa nothing
nitko nobody
niže lower
noć night
 laku noć good night
noćni lokal night club
noću at/by night
noga leg
nogomet football
nos nose
nositi (v) carry; wear
nov new
novac money
novčana doznaka money-order
novčanica bank note
novine newspaper
Novi Zeland New Zealand
novozelandski of New Zealand
Novozelanđanin (m) New Zealander
Novozelanđanka (f) New Zealander
novost news
nož knife
nuditi (v) offer
nula zero

njega care
njegov his
njemu to him
njezin her, hers
nježan gentle
njihov their, theirs
njima to them
njoj to her
njoki gnocchi

o about
oba both
obala coast, shore
obavijest notice, information
obavijestiti (v) inform
obećanje promise
obećati (v) promise
običaj custom, usage
obično usually
obilazak tour; going round, visiting
obilaznica ring-road, beltway
obitelj family
objasniti (v) explain
objava announcement
oblak cloud
oblik form, shape
obližnji nearby

oblutak pebble; round stone
obojiti (v) colour, tint
obraz cheek
obrisati (v) wipe off/clean
obrok meal, serving, portion
  laki obrok snack
obrt (handi)craft(s)
  umjetnički obrt applied art, arts and crafts
  predmeti umjetničkog obrta artifacts
obustaviti (v) stop
obući se (v) put on clothes, get dressed
obuka instruction, training
obveza obligation
obvezati se (v) engage
ocat vinegar
ocijeniti (v) evaluate, rate, estimate
očekivati (v) expect, look forward
očevidac eyewitness
očuvan preserved
od of, from; since
odakle where from
odavde from here
odabrati (v) choose, select
odavno long ago
odbiti (v) refuse, decline
odbojka volleyball
odgoditi (v) put off, postpone
odgođen postponed, delayed

odgovoriti (v) answer, reply
odijelo clothing; (man's) suit, trouser suit, pant-suit
odjava check out
odjaviti se (v) cancel one's booking
odjel department
odlazak departure
odlaziti (v) leave, go away
odletjeti fly away/off
odličan excellent
odlučiti (v) decide, determine
odmah at once, immediately
odmarati se (v) rest, relax
odmor rest, relaxation
  godišnji odmor holidays, vacation
odnijeti (v) carry/take off/away
odobravati (v) approve
odobrenje approval, permit, license
odojak suckling pig
  pečeni odojak roast suckling pig
odostrag(a) from the back; backward
odrasla osoba adult, grown-up (person)
odredište destination
određen specific, explicit
odrezak (meat) steak, scallop

naravni sauteed veal scallop
bečki Vienna schnitzel, fried breaded (veal/pork) scallop
pariški scallop fried in batter
zagrebački (Zagreb style) cordon blue
kosani hamburger steak
odrezati (v) cut off
odsjesti (v) stay (at, with)
odsutan absent, not present
odšteta compensation
odvesti se (v) drive/ride off
odvjetnik solicitor, lawyer
odvojeno separately
odvući (v) (car) tow away
oglas advertisement
ogledalo mirror
ogrlica necklace
ogrtač coat
  kućni ogrtač robe
oko eye
okolica neighbourhood, countryside
okraden robbed
okrenuti (se) (v) turn round
okrepa (food) refreshment
okruglica dumpling
  okruglice sa šljivama plum dumplings
okupati se (v) have a bath/swim

okus taste
oluja storm, tempest
on he
ona she
oni/one/ona they
opasan dangerous
opeklina burn
  opekline od sunca sunburn
operacija (med) operation, surgery
opomena warning
opraštati se (v) take leave
oprati (v) wash
oprema equipment
oprez caution
oprostiti (v) pardon, forgive, excuse
  oprostite sorry, excuse me
optičar optician
orah walnut
orahnjača walnut loaf
ordinacija consulting room, surgery, doctor's office
ordinirati (v) receive patients
  doktor ordinira od 9 do 17 sati surgery, consulting, office hours are 9 a.m. - 5 p.m.
ormar wardrobe
osa wasp
osam eight

osamdeset eighty
osamnaest eighteen
oseka low tide, ebb (tide)
osiguranje insurance
osigurati (v) insure
  osiguravajuće društvo
  insurance company
osim except
osjećati se (v) feel
  osjećam se loše I don't
  feel well
oslić (fish) hake
osoba person
osoblje personnel, staff
osobna iskaznica identity
  card
ostatak rest, what remains
ostati (v) remain; stay on
ostaviti (v) leave, abandon,
  quit
ostvariti (v) realize
osvježavajući napitci
  cooling drinks; (with little
  alcohol) long drinks,
  nonalcoholic beverages,
  soft drinks
oštećen damaged
oštetiti (v) damage, harm
otac father
otkazati (v) cancel, call off
otok island
otputovati (v) leave,
  depart
otvarati (v) open

otvoren open
ova/ovaj/ovo this, this one
ovisiti (o) (v) depend on
ovlašten authorized
  ovlaštena osoba
  authorized person
ovratnik collar
ozbiljan serious
oženjen (m) married
ožujak March

pacijent patient
pad fall
padati (v) fall, drop, go
  down
padobran parachute
  padobransko jedrenje
  paragliding
paški sir Pag cheese
paket package, parcel
pakirati pack, wrap
palac thumb
palača palace
palačinka crêpe (Suzette),
  pancake
palamida (fish) Atlantic
  bonito
paluba board, deck
  sprijeda na palubi fore
  straga na palubi aft
pametan clever
pamtiti (v) remember

pamučan made of cotton
pansion board and lodging, boarding/guest house, bed and lodging
  puni pansion full board
  polupansion (breakfast and dinner/lunch) half board
papar pepper
papir paper
papren hot, peppery
paprika (plant) pepper
  punjena paprika stuffed peppers
paprika (seasoning) paprika
paprikaš stewed meat seasoned with paprika
papuča slipper
par pair, couple
pardon sorry, excuse me
parfem perfume
parizer polony, bologna (sausage)
park park, public gardens
parkiralište car-park, parking lot
parkirati (v) park
pas dog
pasta za zube toothpaste
pasti (v) fall, drop
pastrva (fish) trout
pašteta pâté, patty
  jetrena pašteta liverwurst
pašticada beef Dalmatian style

patka duck
patlidžan aubergine, eggplant
pauk spider
pecivo rolls
pečen baked, roast(ed), fried
  dobro pečeno well done
  srednje pečeno medium rare
  previše pečeno overdone
pečenica baking/frying sausage
pečenka roast, roast meat
  pisana pečenka tenderloin
pedeset fifty
pediker pedicurist
pedikiranje pedicure
peka baking lid
  meso pečeno ispod peke meat prepared under a baking lid
pekarnica baker's shop, bakery
pepeljara ashtray
peršin parsley
pet five
peta heel
petak Friday
peti (the) fifth
petnaest fifteen
piće drink, beverage
  žestoko piće strong drink
pijesak sand

pješčana plaža sandy beach
piletina (meat) chicken
  pohana piletina breaded chicken
  pileća juha chicken broth
  pileće pečenje roast chicken
pilula pill
pipa tap, faucet
pirjan braised, sauteed, stewed
pirjati (v) braise, saute; stew
pisati (v) write
pismo letter
  avionom by air mail
  ekspresno express, special delivery
  preporučeno registered
pita pie
  pita od jabuka apple pie
  pita zeljanica spinach and cheese pie
pitanje question
pitati (v) ask, inquire
pivnica pub, beer-hall
pivo beer
  svijetlo pivo ale, bitter, lager
  tamno pivo porter, dark beer
  čaša piva a glass of beer
  krigla piva pint, mug of beer
  pivo u limenkama canned beer
  točeno pivo draft beer

pizza pizza
pizzeria pizza place/bar, pizzeria
pjenušac champagne
pjesma song
pješački prijelaz pedestrian crossing
pješak pedestrian
pješčana plaža sandy beach
pješice on foot
pjevati (v) sing
plaća salary
plahta sheet
plan plan
  plan grada town/city map
planina mountain
platiti pay
plativ payable
plav blue
plavokos blonde, fair(-haired)
plaža beach
ples dance, dancing
plesati (v) dance
pleten knitted
plima high tide
plin gas
plitak shalow
plivanje swimming
plivati (v) swim
pločnik pavement, sidewalk
plovidba sailing, voyage; navigation
ploviti (v) sail; navigate

pljusak downpour, pouring rain

po about, by, per

po gradu about the town

po zanimanju by profession

po tjednu per week

pobjeći (v) run away

početi (v) start, begin

pod floor

podijeliti share, divide

podložak, milje doily

podne noon

podrum cellar

vinski podrum wine cellar

poduzeće company, firm, business

podvodni underwater

podvodni ribolov spear-fishing

podvorba service, attendance

pogled look; view, sight

pogledati (v) look at, give a look

pogrešan wrong, faulty

pogreška error, mistake

pogriješiti (v) make a mistake

pojas belt

pokazati show

pokladnica (krafn) doughnut

pokraj beside

pokrivač blanket (deka)

pokućstvo furniture

pokvaren (facility) out of order, not functioning

pol half

pola kile … half a kilo of …

polagano slowly

polakše more slowly

polazak departure, start

polaziti (v) depart, leave, set out/off

policija police

polog deposit

polovica a/one half

više od polovice more than half

položaj position; location, site

poludnevni izlet half-day trip

poluotok peninsula

poljubiti (v) kiss, give a kiss

pomagati (v) help, assist

pomfrit chips, French fries

pomoć help, assistance

ponašanje conduct; manners

ponedjeljak Monday

ponekad sometimes

ponoviti (v) repeat, renew

ponuda offer

ponuditi (v) offer

popraviti (v) fix, repair

popunjen full (up), filled up; non vacant

popust discount, reduction
porcija portion, serving
porculan china
porez tax
porezati se (v) cut oneself
poriluk leek
poruka message
posada crew
posao work, job, business
posebno separately; especially
posezona late-season
posjetitelj (m) visitor
posjetiteljica (f) visitor
posjetiti (v) visit, pay a visit
poslati (v) send, dispatch
poslije later on
poslovati (v) do/make business
poslovnica office, bureau
poslovođa manager
posluživati (v) serve
posrebren silver-plated
postaja station
postati (v) become
posteljina bedclothes, bedding
postići (v) achieve, get, acquire
postojati (v) exist, be, be there/around
postotak percentage
postupak procedure
pošta post

poštanski ured post office
poštarina postage
pošten honest
potpis signature
potpisati se (v) sign
potpuno completely, fully
potražiti (v) look for, try to find
potreban necessary, required
potvrda confirmation
potvrditi (v) confirm
pouzdan reliable, trusted
povjerenje confidence
povoljan favourable, reasonable
povoljna cijena reasonable price
povratna karta return ticket
povrće vegetables
povući (v) draw, pull
pozdrav greeting
poznavati (v) know
pozvati (v) call; ask, invite
požaliti se (v) complain about
požar fire
požuriti se (v) hurry up
pramac (naut) bow, prow
pramenovi u kosi highlighted hair
pranje rublja laundry
praonica laundry-room

prašak za pranje detergent (powder)

prati (v) wash

pravi true, right; genuine

prazan vacant, empty

prebivalište residence

pred in front of

predio region

predmet object

predložiti (v) propose, suggest

predsezona early-season

predstava performance; show

predstaviti (v) introduce

predstavništvo representation

predugačak too long

predujam advance, cash advance

predvorje vestibule, entrance-hall; lobby

pregledati (v) check, examine

pregrijati (v) overheat

prehladiti se (v) catch a cold

prekidač switch

prekinuti (v) break off; cut off

prekratak too short

prekršaj violation

prelaziti (v) cross; change, transfer

prema towards

premalo too little

prenoćiti (v) spend/pass the night

preporučiti (v) recommend

preporuka recommendation

preseliti (se) (v) move; relocate

presjedati (v) change (vihicles), transfer

prestati (v) stop, cease

prevariti (v) cheat, deceive

prevoditi (v) translate

prezime surname, last name

pri by, at

  pri otvaranju prozora by opening the window

  pri doručku at breakfast

pričekati (v) wait for

pridružiti se (v) join

prigoda occasion

prihod income

prihvatiti (v) accept

prijatelj friend

prijateljica girlfriend

prijava registration

prijaviti se (v) register; sign up

prije long ago

prijelom break; fracture

priključiti (se) (v) get access, connect; plug in

prikolica caravan trailer

prilika opportunity

primati (v) accept, receive
primjer example
priopćenje announcement
pripremiti se (v) get ready
pristajati (v) (clothes) fit
pristanište quay, pier
pristati (v) (ship) dock,
  land, put in/ashore
pristojba fee
pritužba complain
privatni private
privezati (v) tie, bind;
  (boat) moor
privlačan attractive
prizemlje ground floor,
  first floor
prizor scene
prljav dirty
probati (v) try on
probava digestion
probuditi se (v) wake up
prodati (v) sell
prodavaonica shop, store
proizvod product
proizvoditi (v) produce
prolaz passage, aisle,
  gangway
proljeće spring
promet traffic
  prometna nesreća traffic
  accident
promijeniti (v) replace
propis regulation
propusnica pass

prosinac December
proslava celebration
prostor space, room
prošek prosecco; sherry
prošlost past
prošli last, past
protiv against
provizija provision
provjeriti (v) check (on),
  check up (on)
prst finger
prsa chest; breast
prsten ring
pršut prosciutto, smoked ham
prtljaga luggage, baggage
prtljažnik (car) boot, trunk
prvi (the) first
pržen roasted, fried, grilled
pržolica braised steak
ptica bird
puknuti (v) burst
  pukla mi je guma
  I've a flat tyre
pulover pullover
purica turkey
put way, road; journey
putnički ček traveller's
  cheque, traveller's check
putokaz signpost, guidepost
putovanje travelling, travel
putovnica passport
putnik passenger, traveller
putovati (v) travel, journey

rabiti (v) use, make use of
račun bill; account
računalo, kompjutor computer
rad work
radič chicory leaves
  crveni radič radicchio
raditi (v) work
radno vrijeme working hours, business hours
radovati se (v) be glad of, be happy about it
radoznao curious
raj paradise
rajčica tomato
rak crab
  rakovi i školjke shellfish
rakija (fruit) brandy
rame shoulder
ramstek rump-steak
rana wound; sore
rano early
ranjen injured, hurt; wounded
rashladiti (v) make cool, chill
rashladni uređaj air-conditioning
raskošan luxurious
raskrižje crossways, cross-roads, intersection
raspakirati (v) unpack

rasplinjač (car) carburettor
raspravljati (v) discuss
raspored timetable; schedule
rasprodaja sale
rasprodan sold out; out of stock
rastanak parting, leave-taking, farewell
rastavljen (m) divorced
rastavljena (f) divorced
rat war
ravno straight
razboljeti se (v) become ill
razgledati (v) see sights, view
razglednica postcard
razgovarati (se) (v) have a talk (to, with)
razgovor conversation, talk
različit different
razlog reason
razmisliti (v) think (of, about)
razmotriti (v) consider; examine
razočarati (v) disappoint
razred class, grade
  prvi (drugi) razred first (second) class
  prvorazredan (hotel) first class (hotel)
razumjeti (v) understand
razvijati (v) develop

dati film na razvijanje have a film developed

ražanj spit, roasting spit

janjetina na ražnju lamb on the spit

pile na ražnju spit-roasted chicken

ražen made of rye

raženi kruh rye bread

ražnjići kebab, shish-kebab

recepcija reception, desk

recepcionar (m) receptionist

recepcionarka (f) receptionist

recept recipe; (med) prescription

reći (v) say, tell

reci mi/recite mi tell me

red order, sequence; (seats) row

red letenja flight schedule

vozni red timetable, schedule

u redu all right, fine, OK

redovit regular, usual

remen belt

rentgenska snimka x-ray image

restoran, restauracija restaurant

rezervacija booking, reservation

rezervirati (v) reserve, make a booking

rezervirati sobu book a room

riba fish

morska riba sea fish

slatkovodna riba freshwater fish

riba na gradele grilled fish

riba na lešo poached fish

riblja juha fish soup

ribiz currant

ričet barley and bean soup

riječ word

rijeka river

riža rice

rižoto rizoto

crni rižoto rizoto with cuttlefish and/or squid

rižoto sa škampima rizoto with shrimps

rječnik dictionary

roba goods

robna kuća department store

roditelji parents

rođak relation, relative

rođendan birthday

rok time limit

rok trajanja expiry date

role roller-blades

rolati se rollerblade

roniti (v) dive

ronjenje diving

ronjenje s maskom snorkel

ronjenje s bocom za kisik scuba diving

odijelo za ronjenje wet suit
roštilj barbecue
  peći na roštilju broil, barbecue, grill
  jela s roštilja grilled meats
rublje underwear
ručak lunch, midday meal
ručnik towel
rujan September
ruka hand
  ručna izradba made by hand
  ručni rad handwork, handicraft
rukav sleeve
ruševina ruin
ruta route
ruža rose

s, sa with
sada now, at this moment
sadašnji present, current
sajam fair, market
sako jacket
salama salami
  zimska salama hard salami
salata salad
  (zelena) salata lettuce
  miješana salata mixed salad

salata od rajčica tomato salad
salata od krastavaca cucumber salad
salata od povrća vegetable salad
salata od rakova crabmeat salad
salata od hobotnice octopus salad
salata od liganja squid salad
salata od plodova mora seafood salad
salon salon; lounge
  frizerski salon hairdresser's (shop), beauty parlor
salveta, ubrus serviette
sam alone
samoposluga, samoposluživanje self-service shop
san sleep
sandala sandal
sanduk trunk, case
sapun soap
sardelna pasta anchovy paste
sardina sardine
  konzerva sa sardinama sardine tin
sarma stuffed cabbage rolls
sastanak meeting, appointment

poslovni sastanak business meeting/conference

sastati se (v) meet; come together

sat (wrist) watch; clock

sat (time) hour

u 9 sati at 9 o'clock

savijača od jabuka apple strudel

savijača od sira cheese strudel

savršen perfect

saznati (v) come/get to know

sedam seven

sedamdeset seventy

sedamnaest seventeen

sekunda second

selo village

seljak farmer, peasant

semafor traffic lights

sendvič sandwich

sendvič sa šunkom (i sirom) ham (and cheese) sandwich

topli sendvič toasted/hot sandwich

senf mustard

servis service

autoservis car repair shop

servisna radionica service/repair shop

sestra sister

medicinska sestra medical nurse

sezona season

puna sezona full/high season

izvan sezone out of season

sidro anchor

baciti sidro drop/cast anchor

siguran safe, sure (of)

sigurnost safety

siječanj January

simpatičan nice, likable, engaging

sin son

sinoć last night

sipa (mollusk) cuttlefish

sir cheese

kravlji sir cottage cheese

ovčji sir sheep cheese

kozji sir goat cheese

sir s vrhnjem cottage cheese and cream

torta/kolač od sira cheese cake

sirov raw, uncooked

sitan tiny, delicate

sitniš (money) small change

siv gray

sjajan bright, brilliant; splendid

sjedalo seat

Sjedinjene Američke Države United States of America

sjesti (v) sit down, take a seat

sjetiti se (v) remember, think of

sjever north

skijanje na vodi water-skiing

skijati (v) ski

skije skis

skladište warehouse

sklizak slippery

sklizati se (v) skate

sklizaljke skates

skloniti se (v) take, find shelter

skočiti (v) jump

skočiti u vodu dive

skratiti (v) shorten, reduce; cut

skratiti (boravak) cut (the stay) short

skrenuti (v) change direction

skretanje turning, changing direction

skroz (right) through

skup expensive

skupa together

skuša (fish) mackerel

slab weak

slabo poorly, badly

slabost weakness

sladoled ice cream

sladoled na štapiću ice-cream bar

dvije kuglice sladoleda od vanilije two scoops of vanilla ice cream

sladoled u kornetu ice-cream cone

slagati se (v) get on well, be on good terms

slan salty

slanina bacon

slastičarnica pastry shop

slastičarnica-kafić coffee and pastry shop

slati (v) send, dispatch

slatkiš confection, sweet

slavan famous

slavina, pipa tap, faucet

slavlje celebration

sleđ (fish) herring

sletjeti s ceste skid off the road

sličan similar, like, alike

slijediti (v) follow

slijetanje landing

slika picture

umjetnička slika painting

slobodan free

slobodno freely; at will, go ahead

slomiti (v) break

složiti se (v) agree (about)

slučaj accident, chance; case

slučajno by chance, just in case

slušati (v) listen (to)
  pažljivo slušati listen carefully

služba service; job
  u službi in service; on duty

službenik employee, worker; clerk

službeno officially

služiti se (v) make use of, use

sljedeći following; next

smeđ brown

smetati (v) bother, disturb

smiriti se (v) calm down

smjer direction

smjestiti se (v) find accommodation, get settled
  smjestiti se kod prijatelja (u hotelu) put up with friends (at a/the hotel)

smještaj accommodation

smjeti (v) be allowed/permitted

smokva fig

snaći se (v) manage, find a way

snažan strong

snijeg snow

soba room
  isprazniti sobu check out of a room

sve su sobe zauzete the hotel is booked solid

sobarica chambermaid, hotel maid

sofa sofa
  sofa na razvlačenje sofa bed

sok juice
  voćni sok fruit juice

sol salt

spašavanje rescuing, saving

spavati (v) sleep, be asleep

specijalist (med) specialist

splav raft

splavarenje (na brzim vodama) white water rafting

spojiti (v) join, connect

spojka (car) clutch

spomenik monument

sporazum agreement

sporazumjeti se (v) reach agreement

sporo slowly

sport sport
  sportska oprema sport equipment
  sportske priredbe athletic events

sposoban capable

spreman ready, prepared

srce heart

srčani bolesnik heart patient

pretrpjeti srčani udar
suffer a heart attack

srdačan cordial, affectionate

srdela (fish) pilchard
  slane srdele salted
  anchovies

srebrnina made of silver

srebro silver

sreća happiness
  dobra sreća good
  luck/fortune
  loša/zla sreća bad
  luck/misfortune

srednja veličina medium
  size

Sredozemlje Mediterranian

Sredozemno more the
  Mediterranian (Sea)

sređeno well-ordered
  sve je sređeno everything
  is under control

sresti (v) come across

sretan lucky, fortunate
  sretno good luck

srijeda Wednesday

srpanj July

stablo tree

staklo glass

stalan permanent, constant

stan flat, apartment

stanarina rent

stanodavac landlord

stanodavka landlady

stanovati (v) live, reside

stanovnik resident, inhabitant

star old

staviti (v) put, set, place

staza path

stići (v) arrive, come

stijena rock, cliff
  podvodna stijena
  submerged rock

sto hundred

stol table

stolac chair

stolica chair

stolnjak tablecloth

stopalo foot

stran strange, foreign

strana side

stranac stranger; (from
  abroad) foreigner

strankinja foreign
  woman

strašno terribly, awfully

stražnji back, rear

stražnjica buttocks

stric uncle

strm steep

stručan professional

struja current, stream

struk waist
  uzak/širok struk
  narrow/wide waist

struka profession

studeni November

student (m) student

studentica (f) student

stvar thing; matter
  u čemu je stvar what's the matter
  riješiti stvar solve/settle a matter
subota Saturday
sudar collision, car crash
sudariti se (v) collide, crash
sudjelovati (v) take part in, participate
sugerirati (v) suggest
suh dry
suknja skirt
sunce sun
suncobran sunshade, parasol
sunčati se (v) sunbathe; get a tan
supermarket supermarket
suprotno opposite, on the contrary
suprug husband
supruga wife
susret meeting, encounter
sutra tomorrow
suvenir souvenir; curio
svakidašnji everyday, daily
svatko everyone
svećenik priest
svetak holiday
svibanj May
svi all, everybody
sviđati se (v) like, be fond of
  meni se to sviđa I like it
svijeća candle

svijećnjak candlestick
svijet world
svijetao bright, shining
svila silk
svilen made of silk
svinjetina pork
  svinjsko pečenje roast pork
  svinjski kotlet na žaru grilled pork chop
  naravni svinjski kotlet plain pork cutlet
  svinjska kobasica pork sausage
  kobasica za pečenje/roštilj frying sausage
  pečeni svinjski kotlet loin roast
svirati (v) play
svjećica spark plug
svjedok witness
svjetiljka lamp
svjetlo light
svjež fresh
svratište inn, hostel

šah chess
šal shawl, scarf
šalica cup
šalter (at a bank) window
šampanjac champagne
šampinjon button mushroom

šampon shampoo
šank bar
  za šankom at the bar
šašav crazy
šator tent
šav (med.) stitch
šećer sugar
šef manager, boss
šeri brendi cherry brandy
šesnaest sixteen
šest six
šešir hat
  slamnati šešir straw hat
šetalište promenade; walk
šetati se (v) go for a walk
šetnja walk, stroll
šezdeset sixty
šibice matches
šipak rose hip
  čaj od šipka rose hip tea
širok broad, wide
šišanje haircut
šišati se get one's hair cut
šivati sew
škampi shrimps
  škampi na buzaru
  cooked shrimps with wine,
  garlic and parsley
škare a pair of scissors
škarpina (fish) grooper
  škarpina na žaru grilled
  grooper
škola school
školjka shell, conch

školjke i rakovi shellfish
Škot Scotsman
Škotkinja Scotswoman
Škotska Scotland
škotski Scottish
škrt stingy, mean
šlag, tučeno vrhnje
  whipped cream
šljiva plum
šljivovica plum brandy
šljunak gravel, pebbles
šminka make-up
šminkati se put on
  make-up
šofer driver
šorc (kratke hlačice)
  shorts
špageti spaghetti
šparoga asparagus
špilja cave
špinat spinach
štand stall
štedjeti (v) save, put/set
  aside
štedljivo economically,
  sparingly
štednjak cooking stove
šteka cigareta carton of
  cigarettes
šteta damage, harm
  šteta je it's a pity
  kakva šteta what a pity
što what
  što je what is it

štrukli cottage cheese crêpes
šuma forest, wood
šunka ham
  dimljena šunka smoked ham
  šunka u konzervi tinned, canned ham
švercati (v) smuggle

tableta (med) tablet, pill
  protiv bolova pain killer pill
  za spavanje sleeping pill
tada then
taj/ta/to this, this one; that, that one
takav such (a), such a one
tako so
taksi taxi
taman dark
tamno dark
tamo there
  tamo preko over there
tanak thin; slim
tanjur plate
tanjurić small plate; saucer
tarifa tariff; charge, rate
tava frying pan
taverna tavern
tebe, te you; of you, for you
  zbog tebe because of you
  za tebe for you

tebi, ti to you
  dao sam ti kartu I gave the ticket to you
tečaj course, training; (money) exchange rate
tehničar technician
tek appetite
  dobar tek enjoy your meal
telekomunikacija telecommunication
telefaks fax
telefon telephone; phone
  'besplatni telefon', toll-free number
  bežični telefon cordless phone
  javni telefon pay phone, pay station
  telefon sa 'sekretaricom' telephone and answering machine
telefonirati (v) telephone, make a phone call
telefonist (m) telephone operator, switchboard operator
telefonistica (f) telephone operator, switchboard girl
telefonska centrala telephone exchange
telefonska govornica telephone box, telephone booth
telefonska poruka voice message

telefonski imenik
telephone directory
telegram telegram; wire
teletina veal
  teleće pečenje roast veal
  teleći odrezak na žaru
  grilled veal steak
  naravni teleći odrezak
  plain veal escalope
  pirjani teleći odrezak
  sauteed veal escalope
  pohani teleći odrezak
  breaded veal escalope
televizija television
televizor TV set
temparatura temperature
tenda awning
tenis tennis
  tenisko igralište tennis
  court
tenisice athletic shoes,
  sneakers
tepih carpet
terapeut therapist
terapija therapy
terasa terrace
teren ground
  sportski tereni sports
  grounds
teško with difficulty
težak heavy; hard; difficult
termin appointment
  ugovoriti termin set/fix
  an appointment

tih quiet, silent
tiho quietly, silently
tijelo body
tijesan tight
tijesto dough
tikvica courgette, zucchini
tipično typically
tisak the press
  dnevni tisak daily press
  šareni tisak popular
  press, tabloids
tisuća a/one thousand
tjedan week
tjednik weekly,
  news magazine
tjestenina pasta
tkanina fabric, textile
tko who
tlak pressure
  visoki/niski krvni tlak
  (med) high/low blood
  pressure
to this, it, that
toalet lavatory, washroom
  toaletni papir toilet
  paper
  toaletne potrepštine
  toiletries
točan precise, exact
  točan odgovor correct
  answer
točiti (v) pour out; sell
  alcoholic drinks
točeno pivo draft beer

točno exactly, correctly
  točno (that is) correct
toliko so much
topao warm
  meni je toplo I am warm
toplice spa, thermal resort
toplina warmth
toplomjer thermometer
toranj tower
torba bag
  putna torba travel bag
  ženska torbica handbag, purse
torta cake, layer cake
  torta od oraha walnut cake
tost toast
tradicija tradition, heritage
trafika tobacconist's (shop), tobacco store
trajan lasting, permanent
trajanje duration
  rok trajanja expiry date
trajekt ferry(boat); car ferry
trajno permanently
tramvaj tram(-car), street car
tranzistor transistor (radio)
tranzit transit
traperice jeans, bluejeans
travanj April
trava grass
travarica herb-flavoured brandy
tražen wanted

tražiti (v) look for; search for; ask
  puno tražite (price) you ask a lot
trbuh belly, tummy
trčati (v) run; race
trebati (v) need, want, require
  trebam I want, I need, I'd like
  što vam treba what do you need
treći the third
tren, trenutak instant, moment
trenirka tracksuit, sweatsuit
trešnja cherry
tretman treatment
trgovac shopkeeper, storekeeper
trgovina trade, commerce; shop, store
tri three
trideset thirty
trinaest thirteen
tristo three hundred
tripice tripes
trn thorn
troje three persons
trošak expenses, costs
trošenje spending, expenditure
trošiti (v) spend, expend
trovanje poisoning
trpjeti (v) suffer, bear

truditi se (v) make effort

tržnica (indoor) market-hall, (outdoor) farmers' market

tuđe somebody else's

tumač interpreter

tumačiti (v) interpret, explain

tunel tunnel

tuna (fish) tuna

tura (travel) tour

turist tourist

turistička agencija travel bureau/agency

turistički prospekti tourist/holiday brochures

turistički objekti tourist facilities

turističko područje tourist/holiday/vacation region

turizam tourism

turnir tournament

teniski turnir tennis tournament

tuš shower

tuširati se (v) take shower

tužba complaint, charge

tužiti (v) accuse(of)

tužno sadly

tvoj/tvoja/tvoje your, yours

tvornica factory

tvrd hard

tvrditi (v) claim, declare, argue

tvrđava fortress

tvrtka company, firm

u in at; in(to)

u autobusu in the bus

u školi at school

stavi to u kutiju put it into the box

uboden stung, pricked

ubrus napkin

ubuduće in the future

učestao frequent

učiniti (v) do; make

učitelj (m) primary teacher

učiteljica (f) primary teacher

učiti (v) learn

ući enter, come/go/get in(to)

udaljeno distantly, remotely

udaljenost distance

udariti se (v) hit/hurt oneself; bump into/against

udica fish-hook

loviti udicom angle

udio share, portion

udoban comfortable

udovac widower

udovica widow

udovoljiti (v) satisfy

udružiti se (v) join(up), come together

uganuti (v) sprain, twist

ugao corner

ugled reputation

ugodan pleasant, agreeable

ugostitelj caterer
ugostiteljski objekt/lokal
catering establishment
ugostiteljsko poduzeće
catering firm
ugostiti (v) entertain, feast
ugovor contract, agreement
ugovoriti sastanak
arrange/fix a meeting
uho ear
uhobolja earache
uhodan well-established
uhvatiti (v) catch, seize
ujutro in the morning
Ujedinjeno Kraljevstvo
United Kingdom
uključen included
uključiti (v) include;
(appliance) start, put on;
switch/turn on
ukraden stolen
ukrasiti (v) adorn,
decorate
ukrcaj embarkation
ukus taste; good taste
ukusan tasteful, savory
ulaz entrance
ulaznica ticket, admission
ticket
besplatna ulaznica free
pass/ticket
ulaznina entrance/admission
fee
ulica street

ulje oil
maslinovo ulje olive oil
suncokretovo ulje
sunflower oil
umak sauce
umiriti (v) calm/quiet down
umjeren moderate
umjesto instead
umivaonik wash-basin,
wash-bowl
umjetnina object of art
umjetnost art
umoran tired, weary
unajmiti (v) hire (from),
rent (from/out)
unatrag backward, in
reverse
unfer postupak unfair
treatment
unijeti (v) carry/bring/take
in(to)
unikat unique item
unovčiti (v) cash, encash
unuk grandson
unuka granddaughter
unutra inside
uobičajen customary, usual
upakirati (v) pack/wrap up
upala (med) inflammation
upaliti (v) light
svjetlo turn/switch on the
light
motor start the motor/
engine

upaljač cigarette lighter
uplata payment
uplatiti (v) pay in
uporaba use, usage
upotrijebiti (v) use, make use of
upoznat acquainted, familiar
upoznati (v) become/get acquainted with
upoznavanje getting acquainted, getting to know, meeting
upozorenje warning
uprava management, administration
uputa instruction
uputiti (v) instruct, direct, inform
urar watchmaker
ured office
uredan neat, tidy
uređaj appliance, device, equipment
useliti se (v) move in(to)
usidriti se (v) cast anchor
usluga favour, service
uslužan helpful, obliging
Uskrs Easter
usna lip
uspjeh success
uspješan successful
usta mouth
ustati (v) get up; stand up
utakmica match, game

utičnica (power) socket
utikač plug
utjecaj influence
utjeha consolation
utorak Tuesday
utrka race
uvala cove, small bay
uvečer in the evening
uvijek always
uvjeren convinced; certain
uvjeriti (v) convince
uvjet condition
uzak narrow; (clothes) tight
uzalud in vain
uzbuđenje excitement
uzbuna alarm
uzburkan stormy
uzburkano (more) choppy, rough (sea)
uzeti (v) take; pick up
uznemiren alarmed, disturbed
uznemiriti (v) disturb, upset
uzorak sample; pattern, design
uzrok cause, reason
užasan awful, horrible
uže rope
užitak pleasure, delight

V

vaditi (v) take out, pull out

vaga balance, scales

vagati (v) weigh; measure

vagon (railway) carriage, coach, (rialroad) car
  putnički vagon carriage, passenger car
  spavaća kola sleeping car, sleeper
  vagon restoran dining car

val wave

valuta currency

valjan good; valid
  valjana putovnica valid passport

valjušak croquette

vam(a) to you, for you

van out, out of

vani outside

vanjski external, outside

varanje cheating

varati se (v) be mistaken/wrong
  varaš se you're mistaken

varivo stewed vegetables

vas you; of you

vaš/vaša/vaše (formal) your, yours
  vaš sin your son

vaši/vaše/vaša your, yours
  vaši ključevi your keys

vata cotton wool

vatra, požar fire
  požarni uređaj fire alarm

vatrogasac fireman, firefighter

vaza vase

večer evening

večera supper, late dinner

večeras this evening

večerati (v) have supper/dinner

već already

veći larger, bigger

vedar bright, clear

vegetarijanac (m) vegetarian

vegetarijanka (f) vegetarian

vegeterijanski vegetarian

veličina size

velik large, big

Velika Britanija Great Britain

veljača February

veseliti se (v) be glad/happy, feel good
  veseli me I am happy

veseo merry, cheerful

veslo oar
  čamac na vesla row boat

veslati (v) row

vesta cardigan

vez (naut) berth

vezenje embroidery

vi you

vid sight

video video
  videokamera videocamera
  videorekorder camcorder
vidik sight, vista
vidjeti (v) see, get a look at
viđati se (v) see each other
vijek century
vijest (a piece of) news
  vijesti su loše the news is bad
vikati (v) shout, yell
vikend weekend
vilica fork
vino wine
  bijelo vino white wine (graševina, malvazija, žilavka, žlahtina)
  crno vino red wine (burgundac, dingač, merlot, teran)
  lagano vino light wine
  jako vino strong/heady wine
  domaće vino house wine
  flaširana vina bottled wines
  otvoreno vino wine by the carafe
vinograd vineyard
vinski podrum wine cellar
vinjak brandy
viski whisky, scotch wiskey
visok high; toll

visoko high up, high
više more
  malo više a little more
  ne više no more
višnja sour cherry
višnjevača sour-cherry brandy
vitak slim, slender
viza visa
vjera religion
vjerovati (v) believe
vješalica hanger
vještina skill
vjetar wind
vjetrobran windscreen, windshield
vjetrovit windy
vjetrovka anorak
vježba exercise
vlada government
vlak train
  brzi vlak fast train
  direktni vlak through train
  ekspresni vlak express train
  putovati vlakom go/travel by train
vlasnik (m) owner
vlasnica (f) owner
vlažan moist
vlažnost humidity
voće fruit
  kolač od voća fruit cake

kompot, kuhano voće stewed fruit

voćna salata fruit salad

voćni sok fruit juice

voda water

pitka voda drinking water

izvorska voda spring water

mineralna voda mineral water

negazirana mineralna voda non-carbonated mineral water

vodič guide

vodič guide-book

voljeti (v) live, like

vozač driver

vozačka dozvola driving licence, driver's license

voziti (v) drive

vozilo vehicle

vozni red timetable, schedule

vožnja drive, ride

vrat neck

vrata door

vratiti se (v) return, come back

vreća za spavanje sleeping bag

vrhnje cream

kiselo vrhnje sour cream

tučeno vrhnje whipped cream

vrhunski superior, excellent

vrijediti (v) be worth, be of value; be valid

vrijeme time; weather

vrlo very

vrsta kind, sort

vrt garden

vruć hot

vrućina hot weather, heat

vući (v) pull, draw

vuna wool

vunen woolen

za for

zabadava for free

zabava entertainment, amusement; party

zabavan amusing

zabaviti se (v) have fun, have a good time

zabavljač entertainer

zabilježiti (v) note, make a note

zabluda error, mistake

zaboljeti (v) (begin to) hurt

zaboljelo me je I felt pain

zaboravan forgetful

zaboraviti (v) forget

zabraniti (v) forbid, prohibit

zabranjen prohibited

zabrinut worried

zabrinuti se (v) become worried/concerned

zabuniti se (v) make a mistake, make an error

začas in a moment

začepljen clogged (up), stopped up

začepljenje (med) constipation

začin seasoning; spice

začiniti (v) season, spice

zadnji last; final

zadovoljan satisfied

zadovoljavajući satisfying, satisfactory

zadovoljstvo satisfaction

zadržati (v) keep, retain

zadržati se (v) stay; stay too long

zadugo for a long time

zagorski of/from Hrvatsko Zagorje

zagrebački of Zagreb, Zagreb style

zagrijati (v) warm up

zagrliti (v) embrace, hug

zahod toilet; lavatory, washroom

zahtijevati (v) require, demand

zahtjev request, demand

zahvalan grateful, thankful

zahvaliti (v) thank, express gratitude

zainteresiran interested

zaista really, indeed

zajam loan, credit

zajednički common, shared

zajedno together, jointly

zakasniti (v) be late, be delayed

zaključati (v) lock up

zakuska snack, refreshment

zalogajnica fast-food place, snack bar

zalutati (v) loose one's way, stray

zaljev bay, gulf

zaljubiti se (v) fall in love

zaljubljen (u) in love (with)

zamazan dirty

zamazati se (v) get dirty

zamjena exchange

zamijeniti (v) exchange

zamoliti (v) ask, request, beg

zamotak parcel, packet

zamotati (v) wrap

zamrznut frozen

zanimati se (v) be interested
  zanima me
  I'm interested in

zanimljiv interesting

zao bad, wicked

zaobilazak detour

zaobilazan roundabout

zapad west

zaposlen employed

zaračunati (v) charge (for)

zarada earnings

zaraditi (v) earn, make
money

zarazan infectious
zarazna bolest infectious
disease

zaraziti se (v) become/get
infected

zaručen engaged

zasad for the time being

zastoj halt, standstill
prometa traffic tie-up/jam

zavjesa curtain

zastupati (v) represent

zastupstvo agency

zašto why

zato therefore

zatvoren closed

zatvoriti (v) close

zaustaviti se (v) stop, hold up

zauzet taken, occupied

zavoj bend, curve; (med.)
bandage

završiti (v) end, finish

zbirka collection

zbog because of

zbogom goodbye

zbunjen confused

zdjela dish, bowl

zdrav healthy

zdravlje health

zdravo hello, hi

zdravstveni health-related,
medical

zelen green

Zemlja the Earth; state,
country

zglob joint

zgodan amusing;
convenient

zgrada building

zid wall

zima winter; cold wether

zlatan made of gold

zlatar jeweller's shop,
jewelry store

zlato gold

značenje meaning

značiti (v) mean, signify
što to znači what does it
mean

znak sign; mark

znamenit famous

znamenitosti sights
razgledati znamenitosti
see the sights

znanac aquaintance

znati (v) know
tko zna who knows
znaš li do you know

zračna luka airport

zrak air

**zrakoplovna tvrtka/
kompanija** airline
(company), air company
zrakoplovna veza plane
connection

zrcalo mirror

zreo ripe

zub tooth
zubna proteza denture
zubobolja toothache
zubar (m) dentist, dental surgeon
zubarica (f) dentist
zubatac (fish) dentex, dog's tooth
zvanje occupation, profession
zvati (v) call
zvijezda star (in the sky)
morska zvijezda starfish
zvono bell
zvuk sound

žaliti (v) be sorry, feel sorry
žaliti se (v) complain
žalostan sad
žarulja (light) bulb
žedan thirsty
žele jelly

želudac stomach
pokvaren želudac upset stomach
želja wish, desire
željeti (v) wish, desire
želim I want; I wish
željeznica railway, railroad
žemlja roll, bread roll
žena woman
ženski female
žila blood vessel
žilavo (meso) tough (meat)
žitne pahuljice cereal
živežne namirnice groceries
živjeti (v) live; exist
život life; existance
žlica spoon
žličica teaspoon
žmigavac (car)indicator, signal
žuriti se (v) hurry, be in a hurry
žut yellow

Acknowledgements

The publisher and authors would like to thank the
following for their permission to reproduce their
logotypes:

European Year of Languages 2001

CROATIA

Hrvatske željeznice **Modernizacijom u Europu**

Hrvatske željeznice **Modernizacijom u Europu**

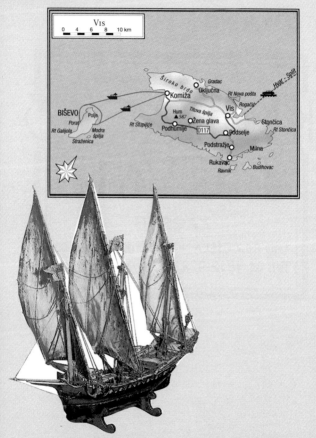

vascha
besedne zveze in slovar

KROATISCHES
SPRACHSOUVENIR

Kroatisch
Phrasen – und Wörterbuch

RVASK_
SLOVNI
OMIČEK

HORVÁT
NYELVI
SZUVENÍR

Horvát
szó – és kifejezéstár

CHORVATSKÝ
JAZYKOVÝ
SUVENÝR

Chorvatský
konverzační slovníček

European Year of Languages 2001

✓ for foreign speakers
✓ for visitors and tourists
✓ for communication in basic Croatian

helpful examples based on everyday speech
Croatian pronunciation transcription

cultural notes to learn more about Croatia
key words and phrases for a variety of situations

Publisher *Nakladnik*
Naklada Ljevak, d.o.o.
Palmotićeva 30, Zagreb
Hrvatska
e-mail: verica.zoric@zg.htnet.hr
www.naklada-ljevak.hr

CIP - Katalogizacija u publikaciji
Nacionalna i sveučilišna knjižnica - Zagreb

UDK 811.163.42(035)=111

JURČIĆ, Mirjana
    Croatian phrase book and dictionary :
<English-Croatian & Croatian-English> /
prepared by Mirjana Jurčić, Bernadette
Kenderić, Verica Zorić ; series editor
Verica Zorić. - 2nd ed. - Zagreb : Naklada
Ljevak, 2004. - (Croatian language
souvenir series = Biblioteka Hrvatski
jezični suvenir)

ISBN 953-178-478-7

1. Kenderić, Bernadette 2. Zorić, Verica

440621082

Printed by *Tisak*
Tiskara Zelina d. d.
Sveti Ivan Zelina, Hrvatska